WHAT MAKES US HUMAN?

The Story of a Shared Dream

Jean-Louis Lamboray

BALBOA.
PRESS

A DIVISION OF HAY HOUSE

Balboa Press books may be ordered through booksellers or by contacting:

Balboa Press
A Division of Hay House
1663 Liberty Drive
Bloomington, IN 47403
www.balboapress.com
1 (877) 407-4847

Print information available on the last page.

ISBN: 978-1-5043-6372-3 (sc)
ISBN: 978-1-5043-6370-9 (hc)
ISBN: 978-1-5043-6371-6 (e)

Library of Congress Control Number: 2016912750

Balboa Press rev. date: 10/07/2016

Also by the Author

Sida, La bataille peut être gagnée (L'Atelier, 2004)
Qu'est-ce qui nous rend humains ? (L'Atelier, 2014)

Note to the English Version

I am deeply grateful to Shyamala Nataraj, who graciously offered to help me with the English translation of my original work, *Qu'est-ce Qui Nous Rend Humains ?* As we worked together on the English translation, we ended up reviewing the meaning of each of its chapters. Our wonderful conversations helped deepen our understanding of the appreciative outlook on people and situations. The result is a better rendition of our experience at the Constellation and a great friendship.

Marie-Pierre Vlaminck drew the book cover. I am deeply grateful for her depiction of the Constellation as a live phenomenon.

My thanks also to all the friends at the Constellation whose stories I tell, and who took the time to review them.

Jean-Louis Lamboray

CONTENTS

PROLOGUE

I met Doctor Jean-Louis Lamboray in 2003. At that time, I was a trustee on the board of the International Community of Women Living with HIV, and I had spent a few years working against what seemed an inevitable spread of the AIDS epidemic.

As an important part of my job, I was involved with and ensured the participation of women living with HIV in matters and decisions which affected our lives. But I began to feel caught up in the complex systemic structures that were intended to save us, the HIV positive people, from the epidemic but kept us away from the process.

In the end of 2003, I travelled to Lyon, France, to participate in a meeting where local responses were to be discussed. The invitation was made by Dr Lamboray. I had heard about him because of his professional career with the World Bank as an expert in the subject of HIV, and also because of his involvement in the creation of the Joint United Nations Programme of HIV/AIDS (UNAIDS). I thought that I was going to participate in yet another technical meeting, similar to those I had attended on earlier occasions—those which had aggravated my frustration over the direction of the response to the epidemic. However, I found this particular meeting different. I was already familiar with the general trend of the earlier meetings to focus on the global response, but I was curious about the shift in the perspective and focus of this particular meeting: to discuss the local response. I realised at once that I had finally discovered the spirit and passion I was looking for in AIDS work.

Ever since that meeting, I observed and involved myself in the major changeover in the scope of that work. What was initially a local response approach to AIDS soon evolved into a successful application in the response to the epidemic. The true dimension of the HIV problem is recognised when we realise that it is not the one and only challenge we face as individuals and as communities. Often it's not even the most urgent, but one among many others that can truncate our dreams.

Our approach towards the issue influenced people's response to HIV. Many of the issues that global HIV experts had sidelined as they focussed only on the solution of the problem began to emerge. As communities began to recognise their own capabilities through self-discovery, they and the outside world began to regard them differently. This motivated the communities to prioritise and address the issues amongst themselves. Soon, the Community Competence against AIDS evolved into the Community Life Competence Process, and that is precisely what this book offers. It neither presents theories nor promotes methodologies. It does not provide renowned experts' opinions. On the contrary, it shares the wisdom generated from people's experiences——wisdom displayed by people who, after recognising and analysing the problems they faced, implemented the best-suited solutions. This book shares these observations, leaving it to us to arrive at our own conclusions about the real scope of this way of working.

Dr Lamboray, with his larger-than-life personality and spontaneous and hearty laugh, reflects much more than the expert and professional that he is. For those who became part of the Constellation, Jean-Louis is the epitome of the spirit behind this approach——or maybe it would be more appropriate to say, behind the way of looking at life and living. His image is congruous with the project to which he has wholeheartedly devoted himself with, body and soul. His open-minded and dynamic personality reverberates around the space he occupies. Even as an expert in his field, he heeds other people's spaces and views. He has such confidence in his recommended process that he knows that its application is not limited to the field of his profession; for him, the demarcation between personal and professional issues is irrelevant.

When the proposal to write this book was discussed, I had the notion that it was necessary to tell a collective story not by putting together different fragments of experiences, but by narrating a story that would convey the complete picture, as if it were one person telling his or her life. I was almost convinced that it was nearly an unachievable task. But after reading the book almost without a break, I now write this prologue feeling that my expectations have been more than met.

It is not easy to talk about a working approach without indoctrination and the academics. It is not easy to describe without lecturing, especially when one's passion is as intense as that of Jean-Louis. But he managed to narrate the stories he came across, together with his own, in the way ancient troubadours did, interweaving the collective life narrative of a complex, changing, and expanding society of individuals.

In his anecdotes——many of them intriguing, amusing, and full of wisdom——we find a profound philosophy of life. His story tells us about strengths and love as a solution to the problems that arise in an artificial social and professional system that alienates us from our social and familial roots. When we surrender to the naïve simplicity of the narrative, we are gently steered into a path of trust in our own wisdom, which we share with other human beings. It is a path where solutions are based on the recognition of our equality as humans while appreciating the diversity of our capacities and our skills.

Reading this story of stories is an exhilarating experience, one that is endorsed by its other readers because it connects us with one of our common basic desires: to be happy.

The contagious and supportive vitality of the author, profoundly emerging from each of his words, warmly invites us to cross the threshold to that realistic experience. We are also invited by the enthusiasm of hundreds, even thousands of people whose experiences are told in this book——or rather, who shared their own stories through this book.

Thank you, Jean-Louis, for this wonderful story of a shared dream.

Maria-José Vazquez

INTRODUCTION

"Me, I am a gangster. The police know me. Until recently, my job was to rob banks and to rape girls. Now, I realize that my life is more important than that!" This is Kasure talking. He lives in Goroka, Papua New Guinea.

Someone asks, "What caused this change?"

"For twenty years, NGOs have come to tell us, 'Abstain! Be faithful! Use condoms!' We barely listened. Then a team of the Constellation came and told me my strengths. Nobody had ever told me that I had strengths ... So now I use them!" Now Kasure visits people with AIDS and encourages young people to take responsibility for HIV.

In December 2004, twelve people founded the Constellation because it was clear that on their own, prevention and treatment programs had little effect on the pandemic. However, the epidemic was declining in a few places——for example, Northern Thailand, Uganda, and Brazil. Here, people had taken ownership of their AIDS problem. They had discussed the issue openly, reflected, and mobilized their own resources to respond to the challenge the pandemic posed to their communities. The Constellation was thus created to stimulate and connect local responses to AIDS, and to complement existing prevention and treatment programs.

At the time, we did not realize that we had embarked on a wonderful adventure. At the end of 2013, thousands of facilitators accompany more than one million people in sixty countries in Africa, America, Asia, and Europe on their response to AIDS and other concerns. Once communities realize how much they can do by themselves, they adapt the strengths-based approach to address other health issues such as malaria and diabetes. They gradually move on to social issues such as gender-based violence and the exclusion of migrants.

What, exactly, is the strengths-based approach? This is the central question that we will explore in this book. However, do not expect a ten-point recipe! Feedback from practice constantly enriches our approach, and so I'll try to explain how it evolved since Constellation began.

When we first started, some of us assumed that it would be sufficient to equip communities with a set of tools to help them act. But we gradually realized that the tools were secondary. The key lies in changing our own mindset from a "needs analysis" approach to one that appreciates, reveals, and nurtures the strengths present in each person, family, and community under all circumstances. Once people realize their strengths, they use them! This wonderful experience has been repeated over and over again, and we are still discovering the power that the change in approach brings to people.

The appreciation of strengths dissolves preconceptions: that for each of our problems, there is a technological solution; that the western world is developed and therefore must develop the rest; that life at work can be separated from life at home; that people can be understood when sorted by categories. When preconceptions fade away, spaces open up for new and creative relations.

Appreciating strengths challenges the belief that there is a technical solution to every one of our problems. Over and over again, we hear, "AIDS? Is there still a problem? Aren't there drugs now to treat this disease?" This belief in technical solutions is not limited to AIDS. Take malaria, for example. The primary focus of international donors continues to be the large-scale distribution of insecticide-treated bed nets and anti-malarial drugs. However, evidence shows that although 80 per cent of African families received the bed nets, only 30 per cent use them consistently. And the rest? People use them as wedding veils or fishing nets, or to protect cows from flies ... or they don't even unpack them!

This blind faith in technology is not limited to health. Take the example of security. We seem to believe that surveillance cameras are the answer, but every day we encounter new instances of violence. Another example is the extraction of water from the earth. This technology comes at the cost of producing more fossil energy, the use of which is a major cause of climate change. Moreover, fossil energy enables users to continue lifestyles that consume more and more energy, and to postpone much needed changes in energy consumption behaviour. On their own, these technologies are not the solution. They must be combined with changes in human behaviour for sustained impact.

Another preconception is that Westerners believe that their countries are "developed", whereas the rest of the world is "developing", and that it is their duty to take care of the plight of the rest of humanity. But once we start appreciating the strengths of our Congolese, Indian, and Thai friends, among others, the Westerners among us (by birth or by mindset) realize how much we can learn from them and celebrate life together.

Appreciation also dissolves the separation we make between work and family. At first we conceived Constellation as a non-profit consulting firm that would sell facilitation services. But we did not anticipate how the approach would impact our own lives! When we started looking at people through a different lens, their positive energy found its way into our own lives.

Finally, we stop putting people into categories and enjoy the discovery of each other's strengths: city and slum dwellers, saints and sinners, straights and all the others, the protected and the vulnerable, natives and immigrants. When we categorize people, we let our preconceptions guide our attitudes and behaviours towards others. In contrast, when we enjoy the discovery of each other's strengths, we uncover the wonderful kaleidoscope of human qualities available for common action. As we free ourselves from our prejudices and place our trust in mankind, huge energy becomes available. Whether we are concerned about AIDS, malaria, climate change, or the future of our planet, there is hope.

Our hope is based on experience. We have repeatedly seen that every community has within itself the essential resources to cope with its problems. We have also seen that when government, non-government, or private organizations open themselves to the strengths of communities, they change too. When Buddhists, Muslims, and Christians unite against AIDS in Thailand and see a way to practice their faith through our approach, we cannot but hope that the appreciation of mutual strengths will enable other communities to act in solidarity based on a shared spirituality.

Can we envision a new wisdom that will emerge from the experience of millions of communities acting from strength? What prevents us from dreaming of the day when world leaders will seek advice not only from their technical experts, but also from the global wisdom inspired by local action?

We can choose. Either we resort to violence to defend what we take for granted as our rights, or we seek a way to build relationships that will enable a better life for all. If you are committed to local action and want to get involved, if you wish to nurture a new relationship between you and your beneficiaries, if you are seeking meaning in your work in the private sector, or if you want to reclaim the governance of your city, this book is for you, and it's for all of us who aspire to leave a better world to future generations.

CHAPTER 1

AIDS Competence Should
Spread Faster Than the Virus

The year was 2004. The HIV epidemic continued to expand as the number of new infections and the number of deaths steadily increased. The efforts of the international community to stop and reverse the HIV epidemic were not bearing fruit.

About fourteen thousand people were meeting in Bangkok for the International Conference on AIDS to share their experiences and to set future directions. Yet a few hundred kilometres away in northern Thailand, local communities had already taken action and had curbed the epidemic. They were not alone; similar stories were being enacted in Uganda and in Brazil. However, most people at the conference went back without learning from these stories.

This chapter describes the failure to incorporate the lessons learned by local communities into a global policy, which set the stage for the foundation of the Constellation.

The inhabitants of Uganda, Brazil, and northern Thailand shared an experience that set them apart from other countries. In 1997–1998, I spent a year and a half in Phayao, a province of northern Thailand, to understand how HIV prevalence had fallen from 20 per cent among young men in 1992 to about 6 per cent in 1997. This was the only the population in the world that had pushed back the epidemic to such an extent. What was the secret?

I invited the main actors in Phayao to reflect on their experience. They were supported by a team of Thai epidemiologists, economists, and anthropologists. Their conclusion, endorsed by Thai authorities, was, "It is necessary to provide services to prevent AIDS, to care for it, and to reduce its impact, but these services are not sufficient. The key resides in the actions of individuals, of families, and of communities in responding to the scourge." Three friends, Dr Masami Fujita, Dr Agnes Soucat, and Dr Aree Tanbanjong, suggested the phrase "AIDS competence" to mean the use of their abilities by communities to overcome the epidemic.

These findings were not unique. Communities in Uganda shared similar experiences with anyone who wanted to listen. They described coming out of denial, making AIDS their own business, and acting locally to deal with it. For example, thousands of people living with HIV organized themselves into associations. They did not hide their HIV status from society. In Uganda, a mother could talk to her daughter and tell her that her aunt had died of AIDS. As a result, Ugandan society acted together to respond effectively.

In contrast, in neighbouring Kenya, people had heard about AIDS, but they did not discuss it as a problem that concerned each family and each community. Although information campaigns were initiated, condoms were distributed, and care services were established, these were done without this discussion, and the country could not deal effectively with AIDS. As Michel Serres says, "Only what is spoken exists."

In 1998, I returned to UNAIDS headquarters in Geneva and shared the report on the Phayao experience. I expected that my colleagues would respond enthusiastically and that UNAIDS would formulate policy recommendations based on the report. But my report was shelved! I continued to promote the idea of AIDS competence even though Michel Sidibé, my boss at the time, relayed orders that I stop using the term. Regardless, the idea had made its way outside UNAIDS.

A few months later, I attended a high-level session on the theme of religion and AIDS chaired by Michel Sidibé during ICASA (International Conference on AIDS and STDs in Africa) in Ouagadougou, Burkina Faso. Most speakers related how they'd adopted AIDS competence as their organization's idea of success, and so Michel had no choice but to use the term in his summary.

The next day, African friends organized an impromptu meeting so that I could share the Phayao experience and its implications for policy, and

I spoke about AIDS competence without any constraint. The excitement was palpable and the vision was shared, but there was no road map for implementing it.

Back in Geneva, I was not alone. For six years, from 1998 to 2004, an informal team grew around the idea of AIDS competence, and together we sought ways to stimulate local responses.

I had met Ian Campbell, and his colleagues Alison Rader and April Foster from the Salvation Army in Africa, in 1989. These pioneers were already counselling local communities in Zambia to address the issue of wife inheritance, a sensitive subject, but it was possible because of their caring attitude toward people with AIDS in the community.

In 1999, Ian was in charge of health services at the Salvation Army International Headquarters in London, and I was able to mobilize a small budget to support the development of national facilitation teams for local responses to AIDS. Faby Ngeruka led the team in Rwanda, and Sue Lucas rigorously documented these activities.

In northern Thailand, I met Dusit Duangsa and Usa Duongsaa, who from the outset had adopted participatory techniques to assist communities. Here too I enabled a small amount from UNAIDS to help them document their efforts.

But I was not satisfied. I wanted to enable the sharing of experience by local actors across borders and cultures. But how? Geoff Parcell's book on knowledge management within British Petroleum (BP) gave me the answer. The company had remodelled its knowledge-sharing mechanism. Rather than call an expert based in London, production teams now called on each other to resolve problems, and they documented their experiences for others. This was what we needed at UNAIDS.

When Lord Browne, BP's boss at the time, realized that his company's knowledge management system could save lives, he immediately authorized Geoff's deputation to UNAIDS. Within UNAIDS, I could count on the support of Marlou De Rouw, who had worked with me since 1998, and on Luc Barriere-Constantin. Marlou had a unique ability to create a safe and friendly atmosphere in virtual networks, and Luc extended his unstinting cooperation.

Unfortunately, we were unable to influence global strategies. National plans and budgets continued to be limited to prevention, care, and impact reduction services; no attention was given to facilitation of local responses. The experiences of Thailand, Brazil, and Uganda——the only countries known to reverse the epidemic in the 1990s——were not taken into account. This international policy situation remains today.

It wasn't easy for me to keep going in this context. Ian called regularly with encouragement: "Hold on while you can, because your support on behalf of UNAIDS helps us in the field. The day you throw in the towel, we'll understand."

One day, Luc found me in tears in my office. Ian had called to say that the Zambian officials were delighted to learn that UNAIDS was supporting national facilitation teams for local responses. But this was not entirely true because the support was coming from me, not UNAIDS, and only for a few teams. The action was isolated and was making no impact on policy. I did not know how much longer I could hold on. I felt increasingly uncomfortable pretending that UNAIDS supported local responses.

The coup de grace came in June 2004. The executive board of UNAIDS was meeting in the basement of a five-star hotel in Geneva. The hall was full. In the first circle, country delegations gathered around the executive director and the board's chair. Representatives from civil society, UN agencies, non-governmental organizations (NGOs), and observers sat in the second circle.

Five months earlier, the executive director had secretly instructed that the funding to the AIDS competence program be cut. However, thanks to Michel Sidibé's intervention, the program would survive for a few months n order to continue, it would now need the intervention of board members, of representatives of my country (Belgium) and of France, who appreciated our work.

On the morning of the meeting, I found out that the Belgian representative would not speak because the executive director had exerted pressure on him to stay silent. Would France speak up? Here is wat the French representative stated: "The delegation of France expresses its satisfaction in the AIDS competence program. In Lyon, in late 2003, we had the opportunity to appreciate the exchange of experiences by representatives from 14 cities across four continents. We would welcome a statement by the executive director on his intentions regarding this program."

Endless minutes passed. Other delegates raised other questions. Then it was the executive director's turn to answer. Would he respond to the French representative? The lunch hour had passed, and the board was ready for a break. Some members were already closing their briefcases; others had started typing on their BlackBerrys.

Suddenly the executive director spoke. "Oh, yes, there was also the matter of detail raised by the representative of France. We assigned a senior staff member to the AIDS competence program, but before I grant him a penny, I want to proceed with an evaluation."

That was the kiss of death. In the UN, calling for an evaluation of a program was the first step to closing it down. It was time to recognize that we had failed. We were not dealing with a personality conflict that could be resolved by changes in staff. The causes ran deeper, and we needed to adopt a different approach to achieve our purposes. After consulting my informal team members, I decided to leave UNAIDS and continue the journey outside.

In December 2004, our team met in Geneva to discuss the formation of an association to promote and support the spread of AIDS competence. There were twelve of us: Alison, April, Dusit, Faby, Geoff, Ian, Luke, Marlou, Sue, Usa, me, and Alex. Alex became our first executive secretary. The perennial fog in Geneva blocked the view, but our vision was clear: AIDS competence should spread faster than the virus. Our association would be called the Constellation. Local communities who mobilized themselves to address their own concerns would form the stars and illuminate each other for more effective responses. Facilitators from the Constellation would stimulate and connect local responses.

Our vision might be clear, but what specific processes would we offer to interested communities? Our friends from the Salvation Army insisted that we develop human capacity, but we were not sure how we would translate this intent into reality. We also wanted to include the wealth of expertise of our Thai friends. Geoff's experience centred on the use of a self-assessment tool that enabled communities to take stock of their AIDS situation, identify their own resources, and use them for action.

We gradually united around a fundamental principle: appreciation of our own strengths and the strengths of others. In our interaction with communities, we would not analyse deficiencies and needs simply so that we could come up with solutions. Rather, through our dialogue, communities would become aware of their own strengths, and as a result, they'd learn to use them to respond to their own issues. They would generate their own vision of success, identify practices that would enable them to achieve their vision, analyse their situation, take action, assess their own progress, adapt actions, and share their experiences with others. We call the combination of this process of systematic learning from action the community life competence approach.

Initially, we thought that Constellation would work like a non-profit consulting firm with Alex as the business manager, and a body of coaches who would train facilitators in the communities that were willing to take responsibility to address AIDS. We planned to sell our services to interested partners, and to help them form a team that could use our approach. In response to my letter explaining the reasons for my resignation from UNAIDS in July 2004, the Aga Khan Foundation invited us to explore collaboration. In January 2005, we started training facilitators in Mombasa, Kenya, from within the Aga Khan Development Network consisting of banks, hospitals, schools, madrasas, media groups, and more. Dusit and Usa opened the doors of the University of Chiang Mai, where they taught at the Faculty of Education. The latter gave us a room to install Alex and an assistant who would support the Constellation, together with Marlou, who remained in Geneva.

But the business model did not survive for long. The association of Congolese facilitators, RDCCompétence, went public for the first time in March 12, 2010, and introduced its work to national authorities and donors. Judith, the brave president of the association, gave the floor to Sandrine Ruppol before closing. Congolese facilitators call Sandrine Mother because it was she who first helped their development when she directed a project to fight against AIDS in the Democratic Republic of Congo (DRC) from 2004–2007; the program was funded by the Belgian Technical Cooperation. Although Sandrine was not included in the session's program, Judith wanted to acknowledge her pivotal role.

Sandrine was the first to use the term "cleansing" to describe the impact of appreciation. "I was not prepared to speak, so I will speak from personal experience. I was born in the DRC; my parents were born in the Congo, as well as my grandparents. You can understand that for years, I've seen you, my Congolese brothers and sisters, through a set of thick lenses. Since I changed my outlook towards you and came to appreciate your strengths. My vision has changed; my whole life has changed. I cannot underestimate the cleansing power of appreciation."

Sandrine's experience matches ours.

We used to think of ourselves as agents of change, but we have become the subjects of change. The energy for our own change comes from the communities to which we relate. To do this, we had to accept (as Sandrine did) exposing ourselves to the cleansing power of our positive outlook on others. But what is there to cleanse? How does that power work? And under what conditions does it work? We will explore these questions in the following pages.

CHAPTER 2

How Much Will You Pay Us?

Mbudi is a village downstream from Kinshasa. The Congo River and its rapids roar nearby. We are no longer in the city, but we have not quite reached the bush. Local residents gather in a garden belonging to a local development association. I have come with Congolese facilitators and am the only white person in the group. We are seated in a large circle; some mango and avocado trees provide shade. Behind us, we see an empty shed meant for pig farming.

After the introduction, we gently enquire about the community's dream for itself. Ideas sparkle. People want to improve the care provided at the nearby health centre, launch income-generating activities, breed small livestock, and grow vegetable gardens. An old woman says, "As for me, I no longer need to dream, as my dream has come true." We're all startled, and someone asks the lady to explain. "Yes," she adds, turning in my direction. "Don't you see this big-bellied white man with silver hair? Have you noticed the big bag he laid beside his chair? It must be full of dollars. Let us invite him to explain his project, and all will be well for us."

Kinshasa is suffering from SOPEKA, or "SOmbelangai, PEsangai, KAbelangai" – "Buy this for me, give me that, offer it to me!" The Kinois might have diagnosed the disease, but it is far from cured, and it extends far beyond Kinshasa! In 2005, Constellation facilitators offered to work together with community members in a Ugandan village in order to roll back malaria, the leading killer of children in the region. The villagers' response? "How much will you pay us?" When the facilitators replied that they had no money, the villagers said, "When NGOs come to raise

AIDS awareness, there is always money. So why do you keep it all for yourselves? Go on your way." The logic is evidently absurd: one needs to pay communities to use their own resources to keep their children from dying of malaria.

At the heart of this tragic transformation from people perfectly able to fend for themselves to becoming passive recipients of various donations, there lies the way international funding mechanisms are organized. For a development official, the biggest nightmare is to end the fiscal year with unspent money. The remedy is simple: organize a workshop, call in participants, pay for every expense, and add a daily bonus. Participants are happy because they can top up their salary, and officials are satisfied that they have spent the budget. In some poor countries, it is not uncommon for senior health officers to spend more time in "training workshops" than on duty. Because these daily bonuses are called *per diem*, the Congolese even call these officials "perdiemistes". In the real world, people pay for their education; in the development world, they are paid to get educated!

Another practice is the payment of large sums to "volunteers" as an incentive to distribute material resources such as condoms, mosquito nets, fertilizers, and so on, or to provide services such as visits to AIDS patients. Often, one community may have several "volunteers" depending on the number of externally funded projects. Some donors will even pay bonuses to potential beneficiaries so that they use the services that have been developed for them. In Matadi in the DRC, a cooperation project paid a stipend to those who showed up for "voluntary" testing for HIV! Where is the respect for the agency of people and communities, and for their ability to take charge of their own lives? What will happen to the beneficiaries when the funding stops? Will the volunteers revert to serving their communities for free?

In 2007, the Constellation introduced the AIDS competence process in communities in six Asian countries, and in six countries belonging to the African Great Lakes Community. The Asian Development Bank had provided a grant of US$50,000 per country in Asia to help us transfer the approach to NGOs and CBOs over a two-year period. In Africa, the executive secretariat of the Initiative of the Great Lakes against AIDS (GLIA) hired us to introduce the approach to networks of people living with HIV, as well as to a network of long-haul truck drivers. The program design was similar, but there was one noticeable difference. In Asia, we had invited all NGOs and CBOs and had explicitly said that we would be able to host participants——but not pay for transportation or a *per diem*. Many national organizations accepted these conditions.

In Africa, on the other hand, participants expected the customary *per diem*, about US$50 per day, in addition to hotel expenses and transportation. When we said that the budget did not allow for *per diems*, some participants urged their colleagues to go on strike. Tensions rose. Fortunately, the network of people living with HIV in Burundi supported our stand: "For once we have a training that will help us. Let us not boycott it." Three years later, the difference in impact between communities in the two continents is evident. In Asia, 473 persons were trained as facilitators, and 543 communities developed their own action plans. Facilitators in each country formed the nucleus of a national facilitation team. Today, the competence approach is spreading independently in India, Thailand, Indonesia, Papua New Guinea, Cambodia, and the Philippines. In contrast, the impact in the Great Lakes region is far more modest.

In many countries, the situation is catastrophic. In eastern DRC, a visitor to any village on the road from Bukavu to Uvira is greeted by a multitude of signs bearing the logos of different organizations:—— NGO bilateral cooperation agencies, European Union, UN agencies, and development banks. These organizations appear to fund diverse projects: "secluded goat farming", "support to AIDS orphans", "support to war orphans", "prevention of sexual violence on women", "fishpond rehabilitation", "rehabilitation of the health centre", and so on. In fact, there are so many signs that one cannot see the name board of the village! It is likely that a single project injects more funds into the village economy than the total revenue generated by the villagers on their own. In such a situation, how can villagers find the motivation to take responsibility for their own development?

To understand what underlies the frantic attempt by development organizations to market themselves, we should recognize that these organizations are part of a broader system where money is the primary motivation. The competition for public and private money is ferocious, and the technique to raise funds is simple. Almost all agencies use the same argument: "The problem we deal with is very serious, much more serious than any other. Without your help, we are heading for disaster!" To buttress their argument, these agencies selectively highlight evidence that will appeal to pity, fear, and guilt. I was invited to speak about AIDS at a panel organized by the American Women's Club in Geneva. The two previous speakers had defended "their" problems, malaria and polio, as the one that deserved the highest priority. I was expected to argue that AIDS deserved even more attention and money. Instead, I said, "The world has enough financial and human resources to overcome all three problems, as well as many others."

The issue is that the leaders of the international community substitute progress in fundraising for progress in solutions to a problem. Upon returning to New York from the Bangkok International Conference on AIDS in 2004, Kofi Annan's key message to reporters was, "The number of AIDS patients is growing; we need more money." The problem was right there. Rather than projecting a vision of success and rallying all forces to achieve it, the objective of the conference became fundraising for anti-retroviral drugs for people with AIDS. There was no mention of the enormous success of northern Thai communities in controlling the epidemic. Ten years later, people in Africa are flabbergasted when they learn about it. Their invariable reaction is, "If they can do it, so can we."

International development organizations judge a project as good if it disburses funds on schedule; any delay is an indicator of a "bad" project. At most, evaluations will focus on distribution of commodities. Were condoms, medicines, and bed nets distributed as planned? The critical question——did the project help beneficiaries to improve their lives substantially and durably——is simply ignored. For example, both the World Bank and the Global Fund often limit their monitoring to disbursement of funds and timely delivery of equipment and services. They are simply incapable of measuring the impact of their grants on people's lives, and the NGOs working with them often have no choice but to comply with this narrow view of development.

It is therefore not surprising that our first contact with a community often revolves around money. People say, "If they have come to visit us, they must have a project to propose. Let's see what it is——and what we can earn!" Antoine Saka Saka is one of the leading facilitators in the DRC. One day he visited the Barambo community in Isiro, in the

Eastern Province, at their invitation. Community members immediately brought up the issue of per diem. Antoine responded that he had not come with a project in his bag, and he would not hand out per diems. Participants began to frown at the thought that they were wasting their time. Antoine said that he had come with the sole intention of discussing and reflecting with community members about how they would cope with AIDS. Most people decided to stay on. At the end of the week, a spokesperson stood up and said, "Professor, we must apologize. When you came and introduced the purpose of our meeting, we made demands that are contrary to our customs. The understanding we acquired this week is a big thing. According to our tradition, we should rather offer a goat to thank you for all that we have learned from you. However, you may have a problem with taking a goat on a plane back to Kinshasa. So instead of a goat, please accept this shirt." When he told me the story, Antoine was proudly wearing that shirt!

What allows facilitators to resist the pressure that communities and donors exert on them? The answer is simple. We believe in our own strengths, and in the strengths of communities. When I was going to return to Belgium from a visit to DRC in 2008, Eric, one of the leaders of RDCCompétence, came to say goodbye. The Belgian project that funded the facilitation team in the DRC would soon shut down, and I was worried that the young facilitators would find themselves without funding. Eric looked me straight in the eye and said, "Times are tough, but we will continue. I promise." A year later, I was at a meeting of the general assembly of the RDCCompétence, where facilitators reported on their activities. Not only had they continued without donor funding, but they had expanded their work! What's more, they put the five dollars they received from communities towards transport costs with trainees and the association's secretariat!

Eric had been part of the group that was invited by UNAIDS to the Lyon meeting that had so impressed the French authorities in 2004. Although his team was unable to get a visa, the Constellation organized a video conference to enable them to be part of the sharing and exchange results of their self-assessments of AIDS competence with eleven other cities. The delegation was enthusiastic. With support from two UN agencies, Eric and his team had started using the self-assessment tool in communities in Kinshasa. The agreement was that the team would not distribution T-shirts sporting the UN logo, because community members would associate it with external funding and ask for their share. However, one of the agencies started distributing T-shirts with its logo, and the team decided to break off associations and continue on their own. In 2006, Sandrine recruited Eric and his team to add a community response component to the project she was leading, and in 2008, Eric became the executive secretary of RDCCompétence, with Judith as its chair. Their team has now trained more than five thousand facilitators to stimulate and connect local responses in the DRC.

You may ask how we find all these wonderful people who are now a part of the Constellation. Here is the secret. All of us in the Constellation are ordinary people, but because we refuse to consider money as the main engine that drives us, we have learned to discover our wonderful human strengths and nurture them as we learn and grow. We dream of a system in which all of us have the opportunity to use our talents to realize our vision, and we must stop hiding behind the armour of our expertise if we are to achieve this dream. In order to become truly human, we must first unlearn.

CHAPTER 3

Before, I Was a Radio;
Now, I Am a Recorder

When I am asked how one applies the AIDS competence approach within a community, I reply, "Imagine that you go to visit the future in-laws of your daughter. You will steer the conversation towards topics that make the family proud, not to their weaknesses. Once you have established a real rapport with the family, their real concerns will arise. In the same way, you don't need a protocol, a questionnaire, or a needs analysis to visit a community. You simply encourage people to describe their strengths. They will then come up with their own concerns as well as identify their own resources to address them."

In Port Moresby, the capital of Papua New Guinea violence, drugs, alcoholism, and joblessness combine to create a fertile ground for the spread of AIDS. We visit a family who lives in a village almost encroached by the fast-growing city. A small, tree-lined river separates the village from a beautiful uninhabited hill. We sit on the floor along with the couple who have welcomed us and introduce ourselves. I am accompanied by a pastor and another woman who lives nearby. The three of us had earlier reflected together on how to visit a home in an appreciative fashion, and this is their first practice session. In our introductions, we avoid giving ourselves important-sounding titles. When my turn comes, I say, "I come from Belgium, I have four children, and I will soon have a fifth grandchild."

When we are done with introductions, the pastor looks for a way to continue the conversation. I can see him thinking, "How shall I start without acting as an expert or as an investigator?" Suddenly he breaks the silence and says, "What are your problems in the village?"

"Ouch," I think. "This conversation does not start too well."

Indeed, the couple responds with all the clichés about PNG. "Yes, the men beat their wives here, girls engage in prostitution, and young men take drugs and are violent. What can we do? All this is caused by poverty!" The energy level quickly falls to zero. It is time for me to intervene.

Pointing to the beautiful hill beyond the river, I ask, "To whom does this land belong?"

"It belongs to our family," our host replies.

"And the beautiful gardens I see along the river?" "Yes, that is also ours," says our host.

"But you're richer than me!" I exclaim. "Why are you talking about poverty?"

Our host is all smiles, and we continue the conversation by exploring his future plans. The energy is up again, and the conversation animated. Unfortunately, it is time for us to leave, but our host invites us back to carry on the conversation the next day.

The pastor does not sleep that night. When his wife enquires why, he explains, "I am still reflecting on a home visit I made today. Would you and our daughter like to accompany me tomorrow?" They both join us the next day.

Toussaint, a facilitator at RDCCompétence, describes his experience. "Before the Constellation came, here is what I did as a peer educator. On any given day, I would go to a community, where I was invited as an expert. Installed at the high table, I would unpack my stuff and start my speech: 'Pan, pan, pan, this is how you catch HIV. Pan, pan, pan, this is how you do not catch it. Pan, pan, pan, this is what you must do to avoid it.' Then I would invite people to ask questions, and I'd answer them. If there were no more questions, I would pack my things and leave until the next meeting. What would happen in the meantime? Nothing! People would simply wait for the next session. Now that I apply the competence approach, it is different. I come as a friend, I sit, and I ask questions. I let people talk about what they have done since my last visit, and I listen. And what do the communities do? They get the information they need to take action, they go en masse to get tested for HIV, and they visit families affected by AIDS."

Alain, another facilitator in Kinshasa, summarizes the shift: "Before, I was a radio. Now, I'm a recorder."

There are hundreds of thousands of peer educators who are trained to behave like experts. They may have received some knowledge from senior peer educators, who in turn have been trained by national trainers. The national trainers are usually part of a formal session of "training of trainers" in a classroom——or more likely in a hotel ballroom, probably after receiving per diems and other incentives. This is the structure of cascade training. As the cascade gets closer and closer to communities, the number of people who need to be trained as peer educators increases exponentially. But project resources are limited, and planners reduce training time and content at the level of communities. The cascade has reduced to a trickle where it is most relevant.

However thin the content of their education, peer educators cling to it at the expense of local knowledge, quality of information, and relevance, and they distance themselves from their own communities as a consequence. They become experts who endlessly repeat the little information they have learnt, together with the message they were told to spread. If they are asked a question to which they don't know the answer, few will admit their ignorance.

José Nkurikiye, from the Burundi Alliance against AIDS, is one of the few who had the courage to admit his ignorance. He describes his experience. "I worked for years in HIV prevention within the coffee sector. All senior executives in the sector, including me, were considered experts in the area of HIV. We taught the workers how to deal with HIV even though we did not have any technical competence. Our instructions were based entirely on some documents that we had read about prevention. We even taught how to care for the sick——without any personal experience in the matter. One day in 2007, I visited a community of former sex workers living with HIV near the market in Dares-Salaam. As usual, I acted as an expert. But after a few minutes, the ice melted, and women began to relate their experiences of living with the infection. Within thirty minutes, we had become their students! We learnt that everything we had recommended so far was the opposite of what was needed to be done.

For example, I had taught that once a person was infected with HIV, it was necessary to take antiretroviral drugs (ARVs). But the women told us something different. 'We try to delay the moment when we begin to take ARVs by maintaining a healthy lifestyle.' The conversation had such a deep impact on us that we even confessed our inexperience. This incident transformed me, and I realized that the answer did not lie in the laboratory. It resided within communities."

In some places, the sessions are so repetitive that communities want no more of it. In 2000, people from the Mazabuka district in Zambia told NGOs, "You came to raise our awareness about AIDS? Please go your way. We've heard enough about it. Let us die in peace." How did we get here? The answer lies in the disproportionate influence of experts on policies and programs. At the World Conference on AIDS in Durban in 2000, the room is packed as Jeffrey Sachs, a professor of economy at Columbia University, New York, advised the international community. "Stop the runaway bureaucracies of the development banks! The complicated schemes designed by those lords of poverty have no real impact! Let us simplify all this, okay? Give voice to the country, and let them develop their projects themselves. Then, install a committee of leading world experts who will review these projects and objectively allocate resources to the best projects. It's that simple!"

Sachs' speech was met with a standing ovation, but I remained seated, overwhelmed with sadness. How could "experts" in Geneva make judgements about projects involving huge sums in countries in which they had never set foot? How could one assess the implementation capacity of a multimillion-dollar project while sitting in a basement in a hotel in Geneva? Twelve years after its creation in 2002, the Global Fund against AIDS, Malaria, and Tuberculosis (GFATM) is paying dearly for ignoring the institutional dimension of development. Many grants have been suspended due to the corruption of implementing agencies. Procedures are complicated: in 2007, NGOs in the DRC had to follow a budget framework that included more than two thousand line items!

Not so long ago, kings would surround themselves with a council of elders whose wisdom stemmed from their own life experience and from that of their ancestors. Today's policy makers are surrounded by experts who base their advice on a reductionist world view. The experts will argue that they base their recommendations on evidence, but they will rarely admit that scientific expertise presents a very narrow portion of reality. Facts that can be integrated into that narrow vision are taken into account; those that cannot are simply ignored. This may explain why UNAIDS still does not use evidence related to the decline of the epidemic from northern Thailand to reorient international policy.

Experts should communicate the results of their research but not take advantage of their authority to make recommendations based on opinions. The first three leaders of the global response to AIDS were respected scientists. Jonathan Mann founded and led the Global Programme on Aids (GPA) within the World Health Organization (WHO) from 1986 to 1989. He had earlier done research on HIV in the Mama Yemo hospital in Kinshasa. GPA was replaced by UNAIDS in 1996 and was lead by Peter Piot until 2008. Piot had participated in the epidemiological investigation of the Ebola virus in 1976, and he had since focused his research on the biology of genital infections. When AIDS first appeared in the United States of America in the early 1980s, it was Peter Piot, together with Joseph McCormick from the Centers for Disease Control (CDC), who warned the world of the presence of a large number of patients in Africa.

But both scientists distrusted the ability of individuals, of families, and of communities to exercise their agency and respond to the challenge. Rather, they viewed people primarily as passive targets of their interventions. This world view explains why the earlier awareness campaigns were based on fear: "Change your behaviours immediately——AIDS and certain death are waiting around the corner!" The message boomeranged; as a growing number of people began to appear with obvious signs of AIDS, their communities rejected them out of fear.

Worse, people were informed about facts that did not fit the campaigns. For example, they were not told that the probability of HIV transmission during one act of heterosexual intercourse between two healthy adults is actually very low – less than one in one thousand. This failure had serious consequences. In many societies, men refused to take a test because they were convinced that they were infected, given their past behaviours. As for those who did take the test, a negative result led them to believe that they were protected by some supernatural force.

Another example: global program managers deliberately exaggerated the risk of HIV transmission through injections, in order to encourage health services to ensure the use of sterile needs. These recommendations were based on a retrospective study conducted at the Mama Yemo hospital which showed that HIV-positive children received more injections than HIV-negative children. However, the likelihood was that HIV-positive children had received injections because of AIDS-related conditions. This did not mean that they had acquired HIV through injections. In the vast majority of cases, they had probably acquired HIV from their positive mothers. The fact is that only intravenous injections carry a significant risk of HIV transmission. This misrepresentation has had a negative impact as people tend to highlight injections as a route of transmission in order to avoid discussing sexual behaviour, the primary cause.

As authorities bask in the illusion of controlling the spread of the virus, they resort to prescriptions rather than information about the facts. People get fed up with prescriptions like "ABC – Abstain! Be faithful! Use condoms!" They switch off while remaining ignorant of the facts. When I teach young adults in Belgium about AIDS, I usually start with a little game along the lines of "Who Wants to Be a Millionaire?" I ask ten multiple choice questions on AIDS, related to the facts necessary to make informed decisions. Less than 20 per cent of the students correctly answer more than half the questions. They do not know the probability of acquiring the infection during a single heterosexual act of intercourse and the factors that increase that probability. They do not know that an infected person has a 50 per cent chance of living without symptoms for eight years, or that HIV positive women have two chances in three to give birth to a healthy child.

The consequence of the lack of factual information is that people are not equipped to respond. Over and over again, we hear people say, "We hear about AIDS, but our knowledge is superficial." The situation is not very different when it comes to malaria. The information communities receive depends on the intervention that the NGO chooses to promote.

Constellation facilitators choose a different path. They stimulate conversation within the community because members usually have at least some of the answers. We also share the facts that everyone should know about the issue. If a community wants to know more, we put them in contact with a nearby source of specialized information: a health centre, a testing centre, a development project, a school, or a specialized NGO. Most important, we do not play the role of the teacher. We introduce ourselves as human beings eager to learn from the experience of the community. Because our outlook is appreciative, we find strengths in each community and discover ways of doing things from which we can learn. Our questions are aimed at highlighting the strengths of the community——their ability to dream, change, share, and develop solidarity. Soon there is no "them" and "us", no "visitors" and "visited", but a circle of people that wants to explore how to tackle a common challenge together. Everyone teaches, and everyone learns.

The Constellation approach is new for most communities. During an initial visit, we often find the meeting place arranged like a classroom. That was how the sex workers in Camp Tshel in Matadi welcomed Antoine and me on a beautiful Sunday morning. Matadi means stone in Kikongo. The city is built on rock, carved by the mighty Congo River that can be seen below. I was expecting to visit a slum; instead, I found a tidy place, with the houses painted white. Mango, palm, and bougainvillea fought their way through the rocks and protected us from the sun beating down on the white stone floor. Clearly, everyone was expecting another education session and had organized the seating accordingly. Under the shade of a mango tree, a high table was covered with the most beautiful sheet available and was enhanced with a bouquet of flowers. Chairs were lined up as in a classroom in the sun. The sex workers were ready for the session. Would we pull a wooden penis from our bags to demonstrate the use of a condom?

Antoine and I consulted with other team members who knew the place and the inhabitants. Would it be possible to rearrange the seats in a circle, with hosts and visitors sitting alternately, without causing offense? "No problem," said the sex workers. Together, we set the chairs. The meeting started. Everyone introduced a neighbour. We shared where we came from, our dreams and concerns, and what we wanted to do in our lives. A joyful conversation followed.

Antoine likes to remind us that old habits die hard, and it is easy to resume the role of an expert. "The old man is asleep in us. He can wake up at any moment!" But when we have tasted the joy of sharing, and when we choose to appreciate the strengths of each person, of each family, of each community, then we progressively lose the desire to resume that role. We can too dream of a world where experts will readily recognize their limits. We can dream of communities who blend scientific information with their own knowledge to effectively resolve their own problems. And we can start now.

CHAPTER 4

No Learning Unless You Act

Meet Khun Pimjai. The beautiful Thai lady welcomes us with a smile to the community centre she has created next to the crematorium in Hua Rim near San Patong in Chiang Mai. We sit on cement benches next to the spot where bodies are cremated on pyres lit between two narrow walls. Every year for the past three or four years, the Constellation has invited those interested to a three- or four-day appreciation visit to northern Thai communities. On this visit, Pimjai is our last host.

Pimjai has been living with HIV for eighteen years now. At first she had to hide her status because of the discrimination of people living with HIV and AIDS (PLHAs) was terrible in her village. One day her father, a village health worker, suggested that she invite other infected people to meet in the shelter reserved for health education sessions. Gradually the villagers realized that, far from rejecting her, Pimjai's father was actually supportive. Slowly Pimjai and her positive friends shed their anonymity. The Japan Cooperation Agency (JICA) gave them assistance to produce teddy bears for export. Although it was important for the group to earn some income, fifteen years ago it was more important for them to meet for moral support and to help each other in daily tasks. At the time, the life expectancy of people with AIDS was less than two years. To delay the onset of symptoms, Pimjai submitted herself to an iron discipline. She would start her day at about four in the morning, sitting on the wall next to the pyre and meditating about life and death. She would follow this with a ten-mile jog!

Over time, other people in the village became interested in the activities of the centre and began to work with the PLHAs. The group's income rose, and Pimjai learned to manage it. Together with some other members of the group, she went to southern Thailand to learn to build a cooperative savings bank. Gradually, the whole village participated in the cooperative. Pimjai's group then decided to stop trying to raise funds from donors—— procedures were too long and too costly, and land outcomes were too uncertain. After a while, the funds from the cooperative were sufficient to invest in community facilities identified by the villagers. They had so much confidence in Pimjai that they invited her to stand for elections to the Thai parliament. Pimjai remarks, "I did not stand because according to the Constitution, in order to be eligible, I should have finished my primary school ... At the end of my speech at the Vancouver Conference on AIDS in ... July 1996, someone asked me if I was a doctor. I responded that before I was infected with HIV, I was a practicing bricklayer!"

At the end of the session, visitors thank Pimjai and tell her how much her story has inspired them. "Yes," says Pimjai, "that is what many visitors tell me at the end of our conversation. But if you really want to thank me, please tell me after some time what you did with this inspiration upon returning to your country!" Earlier in the week, some visitors had asked, "What can we take to these communities that will sacrifice half a day just to receive us?" We responded that except for a fee for refreshments, we would carry no goods or money. After meeting with Pimjai, no visitor had any questions about donations to communities. It was clear to them that the terms of our exchange were not material. And as Pimjai had suggested, they later reported that they had changed their outlook and were appreciating the strengths of the people in their own environment.

Pimjai may be exceptional, but the story is not. There is not enough space in this book to tell all the stories of people who use their own resources and their own strengths to unite communities and inspire action. But how many of us have eyes to see, ears to hear, and hearts to appreciate what is going well in the world? Are we truly learning from the communities that are making progress?

One evening, I arrived with my friend Geoff at Khun Suwat's place. A sanitation engineer and an economist by training, Suwat fervently practices Buddhism. Around 1996, he decided to live in Ban Tom Nai, twelve kilometres south of Phayao and the last village before the forest. At Suwatland, as we call his place, there is no internet or mobile phones which eat up his life. But a splendid light bathes the land that the villagers have given him, where he has slowly built a centre dedicated to light and nature. At the peak of the epidemic, Suwat would welcome people with AIDS to visit and to live in contact with nature, to work and meditate if they so wished. Gradually inspired by his imagination, he built magnificent temples and pagodas with the help of many volunteers. Now Suwat is recognized for how well he counsels people, who now call him Ajarn, or professor. And like me, many people come to spend time with him, relax, and enjoy life.

As soon as Geoff and I got out of the car, Suwat invited us to join him at the village temple next door. "We are meeting to discuss the drug problem." The entire village was in attendance——men and women, young and old, users and drug dealers, police, administration officials, the monks. Everyone talked, and the village put together an action plan to stop selling drugs. On our way back, Geoff mused, "Why can't we hold such a meeting in England?"

Indeed why not? Are Westerners too developed to take such a step? At a meeting organized by Louis Michel, the commissioner for development at the European Union, I asked, "Mr Commissioner, hasn't the time come to eliminate the term 'developed' country from the vocabulary of the European Union? If we regard ourselves as developed, are we not in danger of closing our minds to progress? Don't we need to continue to learn from other countries, especially from poorer ones that cannot afford to waste any resources?" There was no answer.

To reassure themselves about the superiority of their way of life, Westerners are content to accept negative representation of poorer countries by their media. Thailand? Commercial sex! China? Exploitation of workers! DRC? Mass rape! India? Selective abortion of girls! Doomsday announcers reinforce these stereotypes in order to raise money to support their causes. We do not object because it is easier for us to write a check than to change our attitudes.

Having closed our minds, we also close our borders. I remember a conversation with a Congolese businesswoman on the terrace at Ndjili Airport, Kinshasa. The Kenya Airways flight was delayed, and the airline had offered us lunch. I sat across from the woman, and we started a conversation. She said, "Doctor, tell me, why do you make it so difficult for us to come to your country? Today I am forced to fly for my business to Shenzhen in China, although I would prefer to continue my relationship with Belgians. Do you think I do it with a light heart? Why don't you love us anymore?" I think about my friend Miatudila, a former World Bank official, who flies from Washington to Kinshasa via Addis Ababa, just to avoid humiliation at the European border. I think of Lawan Vejapikul, a young member of the Constellation global support team, who was forced by immigration officials to answer questions for twenty minutes after her arrival in Brussels despite having a valid visa; it was only when she thought of mentioning Grez-Doiceau, the village where I live, that the officer let her in. I think of Eric, who was invited to Belgium by the King Baudouin Foundation to train Belgian facilitators but needed my personal intervention to receive his visa on time. And it pains me to think that my Belgian NGO will probably never be able to host a general assembly because too many members from poor countries may be refused an entry visa for no valid reason.

Contrast this with what happened to me in Mali. I was about to return to Brussels when, at the entrance to Bamako Airport, a police officer checked my passport and found an error. The passport showed the stamp attesting my entry into Mali, but not the visa. I agreed to regularize the situation, and the officer escorted me to the immigration office on the arrival side of the airport where two agents welcomed me. I filled out a form, and one of the agents, Fatou, affixed the visa in my passport. "Well," she said, "It's settled. You pay 15,000 FCFA, or 20 euros." I did not have the money on me and said I would call back my driver to pay the sum. "No," said the lady, "Don't call him back. How much do you have with you?" I showed her 5000 FCFA. Fatou reached into the pocket of her uniform shirt, extracted 10,000 FCFA, and put it in her cash box, "Bon voyage, Doctor." Noticing my embarrassment, she added, "Do not worry. God will return it to me."

Her colleague asked, "Do you think your police can make the same gesture to a Malian arriving in Belgium?"

We close our minds and our borders, but we happily continue to export our materials and technical expertise. During a meeting with NGOs and associations working in the south in Louvain-la-Neuve, Belgium, a lady from Burundi stood up to speak. "Why do you send sewing machines to my sister, who lives in a village so far away from here, but you do not even say hello to me although I live right here with you?"

Patrick Viveret, a French anthropologist, remarked at the preparatory meeting of the first Dialogues en Humanité in Lyon. "Westerners no longer love themselves. So, rather than explore their humanity, they seek refuge behind objects."

The thirty-year struggle against AIDS can be divided into two eras, each focused on an object. In the first fifteen years, we underestimated issues of responsibility, sexuality, and human love, and we confined ourselves to condom distribution campaigns. Realizing that these campaigns had failed, we now hide behind the mantra of antiretroviral drug treatment without asking ourselves hard questions about how societies would use ARVs while continuing to reject people with AIDS.

The story of malaria is similar. We measure success by the number of mosquito nets that we distribute. And because we know how to advertise, we transfer marketing methods to the health sector and call it behaviour-changing communication. This does not work. In Togo, for example, at the end of a nationwide campaign to distribute mosquito nets, less than 50 per cent of the children were sleeping under the nets. The figures are no different elsewhere, but the campaigns to promote mosquito nets continue unchanged in many countries. We urgently need to change our approach and understand that communities have adequate capacity to manage their own problems. Because this capacity is dormant in rich countries, donors fail to recognize it.

I have great sympathy for friends who work in the area of international health and development. The bulk of the funding comes from rich countries that seem to believe that their wealth entitles them to impose their way of doing things. Caught between what they know needs to be done and what they have to do every day, my friends constantly negotiate between their conscience and donor requirements. Is it possible that one day they will rebel like the citizens of Egypt and Tunisia, to demand that all citizens orient policy, and not just a few? Will experts limit themselves to explaining the facts relevant to individual and collective decision making? Will a society act to achieve its vision by counting primarily on its own resources?

It is time to put down our burden. The weight of our arrogance becomes unbearable. Whether or not we work in the development sector, we can choose to act immediately. We must simply open ourselves to the strengths of other people, rich or poor, starting with those who are close to us. This frees us from moral judgement, and we are no longer called upon to separate saints from sinners. Instead, we see human beings with their capacities, their concerns, and their dreams. What a relief!

CHAPTER 5

Orgasm Is Not a Crime

In the great hall of the Amora Hotel in Chiang Mai, in northern Thailand, more than eighty people from eight Asian countries have gathered to share their experiences of local responses at a learning festival hosted by the Constellation. The atmosphere is quiet and peaceful as we listen to each other with attention, and we share our reflections about the visit to local communities the previous day. Rabindran, a pastor from a Christian community in south India, speaks about his group's visit to the Purple House, a meeting place for sexual minorities in Chiang Mai. His voice is knotted with emotion. "Yesterday, I was part of the group that went to the Purple House, and I will remain marked by the visit until the end of my days. I listened carefully to the story of Khun Samran Tagun, the leader of the house. What a wonderful life he is leading! I could only admire him in spite of my education, which has taught me to hate homosexuals. While listening, I thought that God could only love Khun Samran like he does everyone else, and I resolved to do the same. That's what I learned yesterday. Upon my return, I will ask my parishioners to change the way they look at gay people."

Rabindran pauses, on the verge of tears. "After the visit, I shared my experience yesterday at the group meeting and translated my remarks into Tamil for my long-time friend who is here with me. My friend looked into my eyes and asked, 'Is what you just said true?'

"'Yes, of course,' I replied. 'It is impossible to invent such a story!'

"'Then,' said my friend, 'I can now tell you that I am one of them.'"

At the same learning festival, a facilitator, Sandeep Gaikwad, from India falls in love with Lulu. During meetings, Lulu is very serious, but at night she is a complete entertainer. Her singing is divine! And with her dancing, she manages to persuade even the most reluctant person to dance! To top it all, Lulu possesses that mysterious "je ne sais quoi" that is enormously enticing. The facilitator shares his feelings with a friend. "Yes," says the friend. "Did you notice that Lulu is a transgender person?" The revelation triggers a gigantic battle within him. In his blog, he writes, "My mind was in turmoil. Weren't we at ease with everyone from the first day? We had become a family and were finding it hard to leave each other when we broke for the day. So would the knowledge of Lulu's identity suddenly separate her from me? I had been told to hate people belonging to sexual minorities. It was very difficult for me to embrace to new sexual identity because of my family upbringing and wrong notions, which say that there can only be man and women and no gay, transgender, etc. But my uneasiness began to disappear that night as I began to accept Lulu as she was. I realized that we are all human beings with care and with love for each other. This is what gives us strength to meet life's challenges. The learning festival opened my eyes. It brought me a lot of friends and a new way of thinking. I left feeling light and happy."

Lulu is leading transgender youth in Jakarta. She uses the Constellation approach to transform her role as the manager of a project to that of a facilitator, helping young transgender persons to form a community to help each other take charge of their lives. In Manonjaya, at the western tip of the island of Java in Indonesia, Lulu and I facilitated a workshop on youth sexual health. The whole community was represented – young and old, men and women, health centre staff and local government officials. We were in strict Muslim territory; everyone was dressed traditionally, and the workshop was punctuated by breaks for prayer. Here in Indonesia, it was clear to everyone that Lulu was a transgender person. A member of the facilitation team quietly asked the old men in the group whether all was well, if that was a problem. "Not at all," they replied. "We learn a lot from Lulu!"

Pontianak is a city of about 500,000 people, and it is a two-hour flight away from Manonjaya. We meet Novi, the secretary of the anti-AIDS committee in the city. The committee includes all stakeholders:

city officials, religious leaders, NGOs, youth associations, drug users, people living with HIV, and sexual minorities. Novi is Muslim and is always veiled when she attends the meetings. But this does not stop her from wearing a blue T-shirt with the slogan "Orgasm is not a crime" in large yellow letters!

We also meet Ibu Ummi Kulsum. This woman is a respected leader of a large number of Muslim women in Indonesia. She is distressed. As a religious leader, what should her attitude be towards drug users? We invite her to visit a community of HIV positive intravenous drug users. We sit on the floor and explore their experience together. Their strengths are obvious: group solidarity, willingness to change, the desire to warn people of the danger of HIV in Pontianak. At the end of the visit, Ibu Kulsum says, "This visit taught me something important. You're one of us; you belong to our community. My children will be the first to benefit from what I learnt today." After the visit, Ibu Kulsum became a keen participant at our workshops in Pontianak, and every morning, she would read aloud a poem she had written about what she'd learned the previous day.

In Merauke, at the border of Indonesia and Papua New Guinea, a team of facilitators practice the appreciative approach in the city and beyond. Ibu Winona is a popular presenter on local radio. She tells us how she befriended one of the hostesses in a karaoke bar she regularly visits. The hostess not only sings, but she also offers sexual services, and the karaoke sessions serve as an introduction. Over time, the conversations between Winona and her friend become more personal. One day Winona asks her friend, "Doesn't this job bother you? I mean, always practicing the same routine?"

"Not at all," replies the friend. "What do you mean by the same routine? I vary the pleasures so that customers keep returning." The hostess proceeds to explain exactly what she means.

Winona decided to try this at home. "Once he got over his initial surprise, my husband was delighted! Since then, he stays at home in the evenings!" Winona winks. "I did not want to keep this lesson a secret, so I organized a meeting of my neighbours and shared my experience!"

The power of appreciation not only changes our lives and the way we look at others, but it also helps us to better understand how others look at us. Joseph is gay and lives in Bujumbura, Burundi. In many African societies, fundamental Christians have fuelled discrimination in previously tolerant communities. Joseph talks about a visit he made to a community of IV drug users. Initially he was full of prejudices, but as he began to appreciate the strengths of the drug users, he saw them not only as people using drugs, but also as human beings filled with energy and hope for the future. His prejudices faded away, and he began to understand other people's prejudices towards him as a gay person. As Rumi, a Sufi poet, says, "Beyond good and evil, there is a wonderful garden. Let us meet there."

Laurence, a Belgian coach, tells how her meeting with young people of Papua New Guinea challenged her ability to continue to appreciate strengths. "Our team was with young boys sharing their experiences with alcohol and drugs, and even gang rape. They said they wanted to change. It was difficult for us to see strengths in that situation, but our team did its very best. We listened and tried to understand the boys. In our minds we tried to imagine growing up in the same way as these boys had. I thought to myself that I may have behaved in the same way. We tried to connect as equal human beings and shared our own vulnerabilities. It was the first time that someone had ever told these boys that they had strengths, that they were good people, and that they could do anything they wanted to change their situation. Soon the boys started talking about organizing coffee nights. They mobilized their entire community. Sometimes it seems illogical to look for strengths when we see weaknesses. It seems less efficient to allow people discover their own strengths when we can so easily tell them all the things that they are not doing well. But our experience is that the detour is worth it."

Unfortunately, the appreciative attitude can be reversed even where it has existed. Uganda is one of the few countries where the HIV epidemic declined over the 1990s. The response started with President Museveni acknowledging the serious threat that AIDS posed to the country and sharing his belief that Ugandans themselves could "kick out the enemy". He did not blame anyone but helped Ugandans recognize that their lifestyle was putting them at risk. Museveni launched the "zero grazing" campaign to reduce extramarital sex, and he made condoms available to the entire population, just in case the string broke!

But unfortunately Janet Museveni, the president's wife, fell under the influence of the evangelical movement and began to campaign against condoms despite overwhelming evidence that the Ugandans thought abstinence and fidelity were unrealistic goals for older people. "We are not sure that we will change our ways, so keep bringing on the condoms!" they said. However, distribution reduced dramatically, and condoms began to rot in warehouses. The acting representative of UNAIDS to Uganda decided to address the situation and called for condom distribution to resume. One day the president's wife invited him to meet her. He went, determined to argue for resumption. But as soon as he entered the room, the president's wife asked her entourage to pray for forgiveness for his sin of promoting condoms! Uganda's success in reversing AIDS in the nineties has been quoted all over the world, but today it finds itself among the list of countries where HIV levels are rising. This story makes me think of the statement made by Khun Meechai, a Thai minister who relentlessly promoted condom use: "In many situations, present a condom rather than a diamond. It is a greater proof of your love!"

We urgently need a shift in outlook from the analysis of what is not to the appreciation of what is, in order to find the strength to resolve economic crisis, unemployment, climate change, urban violence, nuclear threat, family disintegration, and pandemics of all kinds. But to elicit and nurture those strengths, we first need to see them. We can decide, here and now, to appreciate strengths in others and in ourselves. These may not be evident at first, but with practice our blinkers will dissolve, and we will see a vast array of strengths and a wide range of new opportunities to act.

After a five-day visit of Thai communities with teams from Indonesia, Madagascar, and a few people from other countries, we met to share our experiences and reflect upon our learnings. A friend with whom I had started the UNAIDS team in Bangkok was with us. I was looking forward to an enthusiastic response, but my friend embarked on a detailed epidemiological analysis of the data from Phayao that had been presented a few days earlier, and he pointed out areas of concern. He said nothing about the enormous progress that had been made. I felt betrayed, angry, worried, and fearful. Was he going to spoil the outcome of the visit? I was about to intervene, but Usa, who facilitated the session with me, said quietly, "Keep appreciating strengths. What else is there?" By the time I returned to my seat, only half calmed down, my friend had completed his speech.

Another participant took the floor. "Thanks for your brilliant presentation. You are a real expert. As you said, there is probably still reason for concern in Phayao. But you know, we in Asia satisfy ourselves with even a little progress, and we saw plenty of it." Whenever I am about to fall into the trap of judging people, opening the floodgates of anger, I often think of what Usa told me that day: "Keep appreciating strengths. What else is there?"

CHAPTER 6

What Makes Us Human?

"Are we human?" Usa often starts a Constellation learning event with that simple question. How would you react if you were a participant at the meeting? What would you say? Once our participants get over their surprise, they realize the rationale behind the question. We engage with communities on the principle that we are all human; that we have come to share a piece of our human journey with the community that has invited us; that we are not experts who come to teach and preach. That is why we take care to avoid any special treatment extended by our hosts, indicating that they consider us more human than them.

In mid-2009, for example, a few Constellation coaches accompanied a group from the Great Lakes Initiative against AIDS (GLIA) on a visit to Ruhuha, in the Busegera district of Rwanda, close to the border with Burundi. This was an important event——it was not every day that the village received a delegation of people living with AIDS and of long-haul truckers from five neighbouring countries. The villagers had done their best to arrange the modest meeting room of adobe bricks, a tin roof, and a dirt floor. A high table topped with flowers and lined with the best chairs in the village waited for us at one end of the room. We gently declined the seats, preferring to mix with our hosts instead. Bosco Kanani, the Rwandan coach, facilitated our encounter. Even before we could introduce ourselves, he told us (in Kinyarwanda, English, and French) to turn to our neighbour and give each other a hug. After a brief moment of surprise, we happily exchanged a series of warm greetings. Later, a lady from the village reflected, "Through your attitude, you put an end to discrimination in our community. How could we carry on with discrimination, when you demonstrated from the outset your belief that we are your equals?"

Gaston Schmitz left a Dutch NGO to work with the Constellation global support team in January 2007. Like the other members, he immersed himself in facilitating local responses. In 2008, together we visited Tent City, a settlement in Lae, Papua New Guinea. We were about sixty people in all, packed into two buses and followed by a special security car for the representatives from the WHO and the UNICEF.

It was blistering hot when we arrived at the settlement. Nearly thirty people were waiting for us, and Gaston quickly decided to participate as a "brother" in the conversation with young Papuans his age, rather as a facilitation expert. He recounts, "I sat with about twenty people and shared my experience of an STI/HIV test in the Netherlands. A former girlfriend called me three months after we broke up to tell me that I needed to go for a test because there was some risk. I had to ask a friend where to get tested. I received counselling and then had the test. Although I tested negative for HIV, I found that I had an STI, Chlamydia,—which fortunately, was easy to treat. That experience made me reflect on my own vulnerability to HIV and AIDS. The members in my group heard the story with rapt attention and appreciated the common humanity of the experience. Although I was a 'white skin', I was not different from them."

Reflecting on the experience, Gaston says, "When I visit a community as a human being and not as an expert, I feel reassured and relieved. An expert always has to manage expectations. For me, behaving as a human being makes it easier. I simply appeal to my heart more than to my thoughts; I share my own experience and try to understand the situation of people. After such a visit, I always feel nourished and leave with more energy."

Lawan Vej'apikul, the Global Support Team member who was delayed by Belgian immigration, often starts learning visits by distributing paper hearts divided into four quadrants, requesting participants to mark each quadrant with their aspirations, concerns, strengths, and weaknesses. In my own case, I usually invite participants to introduce themselves without mentioning their organizational or professional affiliations. At a recent meeting at the UNESCO Regional Office for Asia and the Pacific, I invited participants to form pairs and talk to each other without any reference to their titles or jobs. My own partner, a Korean, happened to be the regional director. We talked about our respective origins, and thanks to my wife's genealogical research, I knew all my ancestors back to the fifteenth century. They were judges, mayors, and school teachers, and many combined agriculture with a concern for the local community. I spoke with pride about my children and my grandchildren. My partner did too, and we immediately felt an affinity that no formal workshop opening could have created.

In order to acknowledge that we are all human, we have to rid ourselves of the masks we wear – qualifications, expertise, position in society.–—— Only then can we open ourselves to receive what the other has to give, to let the conversation move freely, and to experience our own humanity. Only then can we begin to celebrate our differences:–——we are equal, but fortunately not identical! Once the other person realizes that we do not offer anything tangible like supplies or money, we can begin to recognize and build upon the intangible,–——the relationships that will strengthen us on our path to life competence.

Are we human? We have explored this question with people from around the world: with Papuans, with Amerindians in Suriname, with disabled people in Mozambique, with asylum seekers in Belgium, with young people from the Philippines, and with international officials all over the world. The answers are almost identical. "We are human because we are similar, we are proud of our origins and we aspire to a better life for ourselves and our families. We are human because we love our country and our community, because we want to live together in peace, because we love nature and want to protect it, and we overcome unexpected crises with courage. We are human because we are capable of compassion." An hour or two is all it takes to explore this question,–——and to immediately strengthen our relationship. When we combine our human qualities, we discover unsuspected capacities and affinities that allow us to act beyond our individual reach.

CHAPTER 7

Here, There Are No Local Responses

On this beautiful day in December 2004, the Andaman Islands in the Gulf of Bengal are quiet. The local people have voluntarily isolated themselves from the rest of the world, and today, like any other day, they go about their traditional occupations. Suddenly it is a little too calm, and the birds fall silent. Then the earth shakes. The locals know what might follow: a wall of water devastating the low lands. They warn others and take refuge in the higher parts of the islands, and the tsunami claims only a few victims. The Andamanese avoid disaster by trusting community knowledge built up over centuries.

At almost the same time, as the Andamanese were repairing to the high ground, Tilly Smith, a ten-year-old English girl, was walking on a beach in Phuket with her parents and her little sister. Suddenly the sea started behaving strangely, and the adults watched in fascination. Tilly recognized the scum on the shore; it was similar to beer foam. "Mom, it's a tsunami! That is what Mr Kearney, our geography teacher, taught us at school two weeks ago. Quick, let us get out of here!" Parents are hard to convince, but upon observing Tilly's agitation, the father began to make inquiries.

A vacationer who had just heard that there had been an earthquake exclaimed, "I think your daughter is right." Together, they warned other swimmers, and lives were saved. Mr Kearney had shared the scientific knowledge born out of global experience with tsunamis, and a student had applied it and saved lives. Elsewhere, on other beaches and coastal towns, people had neither retained traditional knowledge nor had access to science, and the tsunami killed thousands.

Responding to the disaster, authorities in affected countries promised more sophisticated warning systems. But it is unclear if they learnt anything from the Andamanese and from Tilly about the ability of human beings to respond appropriately to challenges in their own environment, as well as the need to invest in promoting local responses.

Upon my return from Thailand in 1998, I was inspired by the experience of Phayao, and I proposed to the UNAIDS that I would lead a small team to understand and stimulate local responses to HIV. At an initial meeting, Ian Campbell defined local response as "something that people do by themselves to address their concerns where they live and work". Our world is full of spontaneous, local responses to challenges, but too often policymakers overlook the capacity of people to meet them on their own, and they make decisions as if this was not possible. In a way, such responses are simply not on their radar.

When I presented the Constellation approach to a group of UN officials in Moscow in 2010, they thought it was not relevant to Russia. "Perhaps poor countries to the south of Russia might find it useful. Here, as you can see, there are no local responses." The next day, I met civil society leaders who had been invited to the meeting by UNAIDS, and I asked them to share their experience of local responses in Russia. One example was of a lady who had taken pity on stray dogs in her neighbourhood on the outskirts of Moscow, and she had started housing them in her plot. Slowly the neighbours helped, some with food and others with care, and the dog shelter gradually evolved into a renowned kennel. At the end of the meeting, the officials agreed to support the Constellation, and a year later, Russian facilitators started work.

In Belgium, authorities were sceptical of the approach. "Your approach seems better suited for groups in poor countries. Here, the focus is either on a mass based, on an individual based approach." Yet Belgium, a country of ten million, has no less than 120,000 registered non-profit organizations (and many other informal ones), leading us to believe that the approach can work here too.

Although it is true that the sense of community tends to disappear as societies urbanize and modernize, we must recognize that the members in these societies continue to remain human, and they continue to seek to build relationships in newer ways, even virtually. This may explain the enormous success of social networking sites such as Facebook. At the same time, there is an increasing trend to reconnect with neighbours through, for example, neighbourhood and street festivals in Belgium, or through promoting common spaces for communities to meet, as in the high-rise towers that have replaced the kampungs (villages) in Singapore. However, it is also true that in many situations, communities lack confidence in their own ability to act.

Earlier in this book, we explored the mobilizing power of appreciation. We will now discuss how the appreciation of each other's strengths has become the Constellation's DNA.

CHAPTER 8

SALT——Our DNA

SALT—— is the term we use for the approach of the Constellation. What is SALT, and how did it evolve? In 1999, I was with the local response unit at UNAIDS headquarters in Geneva, driven by the need to learn from the unique experience of communities of northern Thailand, and to benefit other communities in Africa and elsewhere in their responses to HIV and AIDS. On the recommendation of a friend, we invited an English consultant, who offered a single suggestion at the end of a day's visit. "Adapt the example of Support to Action Learning Teams (SALT) in the UK." These teams connect to all services that are called upon during catastrophes such as blazes, train accidents, terrorist attacks, or floods. They meet after the occurrence of a disaster to discuss, reflect, and take action during the emergency, as well as improving systems to prevent disasters. We were all excited by the idea!

I immediately called Ian, who was intrigued. He explored it with the team from the Salvation Army that was stimulating and accompanying local responses to AIDS in Africa. They returned with a list of verbs associated with each of the letters in the word. To the S for "Support", they added "Stimulate". To the A for "Action", they added "Analyse" and "Appreciate". To the L for "Learning", they added "Link". To the T for "Team", they added "Transform" and "Transfer". Initially, I preferred the simpler definition used by our English visitor, but over time we realized that the words used by Ian and his team described the essence, the DNA, of the Constellation approach, even as we continued to reflect on its meanings.

Early on, we associated SALT with the first visit we made to a community and the process of getting to know each other. Our goal was to interact with the community, explore its strengths and its concerns, and perhaps, offer to accompany the local response to those concerns. We returned to that community only if they invited us back. It took many of us time——years, actually——to associate SALT with the entire interaction we have with communities, and not with just that first visit.

While thinking about how our understanding of SALT evolved, I remember the day in January 2008 when the Constellation support team met in our living room in Grez-Doiceau to receive Brigitte, the marketing manager for Europe, for a large cosmetic firm. Brigitte was going to help us examine our brand. "Think of the Constellation support team as a person. What would be that person's job?" she asked.

Without consulting each other, we answered in unison, "A midwife!" As midwives, Constellation facilitators accompany the birth of a project that is not theirs. They don't give it their name, and later on, nobody will remember them. Think of the Socratic method,——the art of helping to express what is already known.——That's what the "S" in Stimulate represents for us. In conversations with community members, facilitators ask questions that allow members to recognize their strengths and use them.

Reflecting on the letter "A", like Sandrine we have discovered the power of appreciating strengths. During conversations with a community, we immerse ourselves in the interaction, and the separation between "we" and "them" tends to blur and melt into "us". Like children, we see reality as it is:——what is beautiful, just, and true. When we appreciate without analysis and sense without judgement, it is almost an aesthetic experience. For example, when enjoying a beautiful piece of music, I am fully immersed in the experience. I do not analyse what makes it beautiful; although analysis is possible, it comes after the experience. Appreciating strengths is similar.——We do not ask people to describe their strengths; we interact with them in such a way so that these become obvious. The process of reflection at the end of the conversation helps to name them.

The next letter in SALT, "L", is for learning and link. Remember Novi, the lady who served on the anti-AIDS committee in Pontianak city in Indonesia? Upon returning from their first SALT visit, a group of eighty people (including Novi) were reflecting on their experience. They had interacted with drug users, street children, transgender persons, persons living with HIV, and others. When they spoke, their frustration was palpable. They had not been able to refrain from judging and analysing, and as a result, they were unable to carry on a normal conversation with the people they had met. During her visit to a detention centre for young offenders, one team member asked, "I have kids your age. What advice can you give them so they do not fall into the terrible situation that is yours?" Imagine the time and effort it would have taken to rekindle the morale of the youngsters! Reflecting the mood of the team, another member said forcefully, "I have participated in workshops for years, but I've never experienced a facilitation of such poor quality. How could you let us go out there without a structure, without a protocol?" I can still hear the accusation in her tone.

The atmosphere at the facilitators' session was just as bleak. "Should we not have a questionnaire to at least guide us?" I let the facilitators express their anxiety, but I did my best to not get sucked into the prevailing sense of frustration.

After a while, Novi responded, "Well, in these conditions each of must develop his or her own structure!" That is exactly what the members did to prepare for their visits on the following day. They decided to abandon their attitudes as experts, and they engaged instead as human beings in their interactions with community members. When they returned this time around, the atmosphere was jovial.

At the Constellation, there is no learning without application in other contexts. When people in the community gain confidence in their own resources, they tell us, "Thank you for allowing us to realize our strengths. We will not wait anymore for experts or for donors before we act!" Facilitators often thank community members by saying, "Thank you very much. We learned a lot!"

I also wonder what mysterious chance led us to understand that the "T" should stand for transfer, as well as for team. At the end of her visit to the association of former drug users living with HIV, Ibu Ummi Kulsum, the Muslim leader in Pontianak, decided to do exactly that. Appreciating the solidarity of the community, she concluded, "You are one of us, and the primary beneficiaries of what I just learned will be my family." Ibu

Kulsum did not merely bring home a protocol——she returned with a principle: Adapt and implement in your own context! We can assume that her experience will benefit many of her 200,000 followers.

But how do we deal with the "real" needs of the community? Once we have appreciated strengths and learned from the communities, do we simply leave them alone with their needs? No. We link them with others who can help. For example, a team of Congolese facilitators visited an association of people living with AIDS in Kinshasa. One member of the association remarked, "We will soon die. The Global Fund has removed the NGO that used to give us our anti-retroviral drugs from its list. Our last consignment is almost exhausted. We explored with the National Programme and other NGOs that care for AIDS patients, but everywhere they tell us, 'Come back later. We can no longer enrol new patients.'

One facilitator responded, 'Do you know that not far from here, the Centre Kimbanguiste has a large stock of ARVs that will soon be obsolete?' The members did not know. The facilitation team quickly established the link, and members were able to continue treatment.

More recently, we have started thinking about SALT in the reverse order:——TLAS! We find that everything flows much more easily when we start with our intent to transfer what we learn from communities into our own context. For example, instead of asking long-distance truckers what they do to protect themselves from AIDS, I express my own needs. "I travel as much as you. I travel by plane, and you by truck. But in the evening, our loneliness is the same. What can you advise me from your experience?" Because I express a request, the response is very different. The truckers now want to help me rather than to respond to a question about them. And because the questions are genuinely appreciative, and I try to learn from their experience, they also stimulate the people I visit. While they think about how best to respond to my request, they also strengthen their own principles for action, and at the end of the conversation, we both emerge stronger.

The word "transform" is another way we understand the "T" in SALT. Is transfer possible without the personal transformation of the person who transfers? Our experience tells us that it is not. Joao Arnaldo Vembane, from Handicap International in Mozambique, describes the sentiment of many stakeholders in the fight against AIDS when they are first faced

43

with the SALT approach. "At the beginning of my involvement with this [Constellation] process, I thought it was craziness to think that we may learn from the illiterate communities. I and others like me were the experts and could change the course of whatever vulnerability. However, when we look at the facts, how much we are really changing the trends when we act as experts becomes highly disputable. Nothing is happening. Something new or different should be tried."

In April 2011, at the end of a long winter in Kazan, the capital of Tatarstan eight miles east of Moscow, the dirty snow is melting. On the invitation of UNAIDS Europe, we initiate a group of Russian facilitators to the SALT approach. Among them is Sveta, a tiny woman known throughout Russia for her courage in disclosing her HIV status and organizing a caravan to raise AIDS awareness in this vast country. Earlier that morning, we had enjoyed her clear presentation to the Tatarstan authorities. That night, thanks to her, we were invited to a meeting of the local Rotary Club. The club members expect me (as the expert) to make a presentation. Instead, we organize them into groups of three to four and request they to introduce themselves by sharing something they are proud of. After a moment of surprise, they start the introductions. Soon the conversation is lively, and the president has difficulty in ending the session so that dinner may be served. At the end of the meal, Ian (him again!) pulls out a traditional salt box from his pocket. The box had been given to him by a lady at the end of a SALT visit to St Petersburg, ten years earlier, and Ian establishes a parallel between the table salt and the SALT approach. Taking the floor after Ian, the club's chairman describes the salt ceremony still practiced in this region, and he invites us to share something we enjoy with the group while holding the box of salt in front of us. At the end, we each take a pinch of salt and put it on our tongues, and the president observes, "Like salt, SALT is a guarantee of authenticity and longevity." As the meeting ends, the Rotarians commit to helping Sveta and her team to facilitate local responses to HIV and AIDS in Tatarstan!

CHAPTER 9

Reclaiming Our Right to Dream

"Jean-Louis, let us write the universal declaration on the right to dream together," says Hakim, the dean of the Faculty of Science at Hassan II University in Casablanca. We are the workshop on the development of AIDS competence in Morocco, and he has just completed a group assignment. "Imagine that it is 2035, and that Morocco has successfully responded to AIDS. Draw something that symbolizes the success, and describe in ten sentences what Moroccans did to succeed." The group, comprised of people from all over the country, takes the best part of the afternoon to complete the assignment. Hakim is radiant. "It's been so long since we last dreamed. We are so busy, so stressed! Thank you for having opened this space."

Isn't it true that we don't dream alone anymore, let alone in groups? When we ask people in Europe to share their dreams, they often respond, "I do not share my dreams. They are private."

"Okay," we respond. "No problem. Feel free to share what you want, and keep the rest in your secret garden." Maybe at a fundamental level, it takes courage to dream. After all, we can't fail as long as we don't define success——but we can't win either!

In the early days of the Constellation, building a common dream was not part of our process. If a community invited us back after an initial visit, we would immediately facilitate a structured discussion on AIDS competence based on a self-assessment framework. The "aha" moment came during a neighbourhood meeting in Matadi, the port city on the Congo River. The RDCCompétence facilitators and I were waiting in a tin shelter for our meeting to start. Below, we could see the cranes in the port. To our left, downstream, the river entered the hell's cauldron, a large whirlpool where boats would be lost forever. On the right, upstream where the cataracts ended, the Portuguese explorer Diego Cao had stopped his exploration and asked the people, "What do you call this river?"

"Nzadi!——This is the river," they answered. And that is the origin of the word Zaïre, which briefly replaced Congo as the name of this huge country.

Our hosts arrived, and the meeting began. Our newly initiated facilitator introduced himself and the visitors, and people listened attentively. He was not comfortable and talked in circles as he sought a way to gently introduce the topic of AIDS into the conversation. At last he announced, "Today we will take stock of AIDS in our community." The discomfort was palpable, although it would disappear as the conversation picked up. At the action review, after the meeting, we agreed to explore the idea of introducing the concept of a common dream before we started any conversation on the current situation.

At Camp Tshel the next day, we met with a group of sex workers. The atmosphere was relaxed, and they expected nothing more than another presentation on AIDS, as well as a demonstration of condom application. Instead, we began by asking them to share the dreams they had for themselves. "For me," said one woman, "I'm almost finished with this work. I will soon have saved enough money to open a shop in Kinshasa." Another shared, "I'm in love with a sailor who docks regularly in Matadi. I think that next time, he will take me with him." A third woman said, "Everything goes well for me because I am older."

The men listened, standing in a circle around us. A woman asked them, "Why don't you say something? What are your dreams for the future?" The young men who accompany the girls on the boats to help translate and negotiate their services said that they want to set up a real business for their services. The owner of the compound shared that he wanted to install running water in all the houses. An older man, a local judge, said, "As for me, I have reached my dream. I am very happy to live in this community!"

These were the early days of the Constellation, and many of us had not thought of sharing our own aspirations because we still thought of ourselves as external facilitators. But at this meeting, we found it easy to share our concern that AIDS might jeopardize the dreams of the community. Everyone agreed that it was important to discuss the issue with all the sex workers. "You've chosen a bad day for such an important discussion. It's Sunday, and a lot of girls are still sleeping. Please come again, and you will see that all of us will be there." At the next meeting, the Camp Tshel community adopted an action plan to deal with AIDS, one aspect of which was a decision being to volunteer in large numbers to take an HIV test.

When we visit a community, we invite members to formulate their own definitions of success when seen in the long term. When communities focus on the short and medium term, they tend to restrict their aspirations. When we situate the dream in the long term, we free ourselves from self-imposed constraints. For example, facilitators of BelCompétence, our Belgian member organization, drew a circle of hands of different colours to express their dream of the Belgium of tomorrow. But this dream is impossible to realize in the short term.

We have also learned that the dream evolves over time. At first, when communities dream of a successful response to AIDS, they tend to limit their aspirations to tangible aspects such as access to health care and condoms. Later, when they revisit their dream after they have taken some action to achieve it, they tend to prioritize other equally important but less tangible aspects, such as dialogue within the family, reduction of alcohol consumption, inclusion of families affected by AIDS, harmonious relations between men and women, respect for and inclusion of sexual minorities, mobilization of the community's own resources, and development of its management capacities.

The dream is the glue that binds a community, whether recently formed to address a specific concern, or already established. When people formulate their dreams, they immediately feel closer to each other. They discover common aspirations and concerns and discover new dimensions to their own dreams, thanks to the contributions of others. They realize what they can do together to make progress. The collective dream opens the way for actions that no individual can undertake alone.

The formulation of the dream leads naturally into action. Some communities act immediately. Risya Kori was with the United Nations

Fund for Population Activities (UNFPA) and served as the liaison between the Constellation and leaders of three Indonesian cities who visited northern Thailand to appreciate local responses to AIDS. After leaving the UNFPA to join UNDP (United Nations Development Program), she applied our appreciative approach to her new job, which was related to the development of human rights, especially for women.

Describing her experience, she says, "When people start talking, amazing things can happen. One day I went to Pulooro, a small village in Konawe district in south-east Sulawesi. The village was sixteen kilometres from the main road, and we had to hire motorcycle taxis to get there because the road could not accommodate a car. There was no school in Pulooro, the health centre offered limited services, and electricity was in short supply. Most people made their living from agriculture. Nobody seemed interested in improving access to the village, and children had to walk a long way to reach their school, which was located outside the village. Although they were enthusiastic in the beginning, some dropped out because they were tired of the daily walk.

"The village chief lived differently,——in a mansion near the main road, with two cars parked in his garage. Because he was involved in the illegal exploitation of the village forest, he had done everything to prevent people from visiting Pulooro. Soon after my visit, I suggested to a friend who was already working with that village that together we invite the community to generate their vision of their future so that they could act on it. On the day of the meeting, we arrived too late to arrange the room, and we were greeted by hundreds of community members seated like in a classroom, with the chief and his team sitting in front, facing them. We knew that the community members had been instructed to remain silent and that the chief had appointed a spokesman to answer our questions. Tired of hearing the spokesperson's voice, my friend suddenly took the floor and said, 'We are here to listen. What are your dreams for your community? If you dream that your children go to school, and that you can sell your farm products outside, you have that power to do that here in this community!'

"After moment's silence, a woman stood up and began to talk about her concerns and her dream for the community. Others followed her courageous example and spoke. At the end of the visit, the room was filled with energy. For the first time in years, the villagers could share their concerns and their dreams. Six months later, my friend told me that the woman who had spoken first had won the elections. Soon after, she replaced the village chief, and the government has already repaired the village road."

When I read the story of Pulooro on our exchange platform online, I wondered if the time was ripe for us in Europe to reclaim the management of our own cities rather than rely on local governments. We can generate our own vision of the future for all of us to achieve.

Although the Pulooro community could act on their dream, in other cases a facilitator accompanies the community in the translation of its dream into reality. John Piermont Montilla, of Kabataang Gabay sa Positibong Pamumuhay (Peers for Positive Living) in the Philippines, shares his experience. "I am a survivor of trafficking in the areas of prostitution and illicit drug trade, and the organization which I built works in the southern Philippines with children in difficult circumstances – child labour, exploitation, and prostitution! I looked for a way to help children to change their behaviour using my own experience. As a survivor myself, I inspire them of the power of dreams. I have found that helping children to build or rebuild their dreams allows them to find a direction in their lives and move forward,——just like I did when I was on the streets. What we have done in our organization is effective. Every child has a dream. Facilitating in sharing dreams using the SALT approach enables them to achieve a shared vision. This gives them a sense of belonging to a community that believes that each dream can come true through helping each other.

"While sharing our individual dreams and forming of our collective dreams, we did not directly discuss about the risk of HIV infection. But as the conversations went along, the children began to talk about the risk behaviours they were taking in relation to HIV. We then facilitated self-assessment of their risks using a grid specific to their peer-sanctioned practices, and they set their own targets for change for each risk behaviour identified. We call this tool the River of Life Initiative (ROLi) toolkit. Now because of the tool, they are no longer embarrassed to talk about their behaviours, not only with peers but also with community leaders. They proudly state, 'I want to change this behaviour.' This puts pressure on leaders to review the services they provide to the children, and to tailor them in support of children and youth so that they address their unmet sexual health needs.

"Before this process, people did not trust children, especially those engaging in high-risk behaviours. Now, adults who see them and listen to the milestones of change they share during dialogues; they start to restore the trust they lost due to the stigma attached to their social conditions. Our optimism for these deeply misunderstood children inspires them too. They think, 'Even though I am like this there are still people who believe in me.' The children have now transitioned to formal schooling, and some go to vocational schools. We link those not literate enough to go to school with non-exploitative, income-generating opportunities. We simply facilitate access and agree on how to keep in touch. It has been a very successful initiative. Not only have the children become more AIDS competent, but they are now more life competent!"

CHAPTER 10

Working Together——Key Practices

Once a community has built its dream, facilitators invite members to reflect and identify what is needed to achieve it. The list is often long, and it takes skill to group the actions into main practices. Whatever their concern——AIDS, malaria, diabetes, social peace, domestic violence, reproductive health, and so on——practices can be summarized as follows.

1. We know what problem affects us, and how.
2. We involve affected families in our thinking and in our actions.
3. We prevent the problem (this general practice is often divided into specific prevention practices).
4. We ensure that all those who are affected by the problem receive attention and care.
5. We review our progress and adapt our actions.
6. We draw on the experience of others and share our own.
7. We nurture our relationships so that we can live to our full potential, irrespective of our differences.
8. We work in such a way that everyone can contribute.
9. We mobilize our own resources first and seek external resources only if necessary.

Not long ago, facilitators would carry a predetermined list of practices tested in other countries. It was only in 2008 in Mumbai, India, that I really understood the crucial need for communities to generate their own framework for action if they had to feel a sense of ownership about the process and initiate action. The meeting, supported by the Asian Development Bank, had brought together some sixty members of associations and NGOs to whom we had transferred our approach, and people shared their experience. But something wasn't working. We had suggested that the interactions should be based on the self-assessment practices, but the framework was in English. We said, "Please gather into language groups and describe the practices that lead to AIDS competence." There were no less than seven language groups, and participants got to work. A few hours later, as they were about to finish, people from Karnataka state suddenly got up to dance and sing in Kannada, their native language. Other groups spontaneously followed in their own languages——Hindi, Urdu, Tamil, and so on. The last group sang in English, and everyone participated. I have no words to convey the joy of the moment, and the energy spread from Mumbai to fuel the development of AIDS competence in India.

Since that experience, we are careful not to impose our framework on any community. Rebeka Sultana is a medical doctor from Bangladesh, where she used to run a family health centre. She left Bangladesh to follow her husband to Indonesia, became interested in the life competence process, and adapted it to work with communities to address gender-related concerns. In June 2010, we joined a team of Indonesian facilitators in Jayapura, the capital of Papua on the Indonesian part of the island. Volcanic mountains plunged directly into the sea and defined the convoluted coasts and lakes, which were bordered by lush vegetation. But in this idyllic setting, domestic violence is common, and community members are concerned. Describing her interaction, Rebeka wrote, "When we met with community members, we realized that we had to rid ourselves of the concepts of gender and gender-based violence. We said to ourselves, Let us learn from their experience. At the end of the week, the community had developed its own evaluation framework in its own language. You and me, we have the professional experience to develop a wonderful framework for self-assessment, but it does not necessarily reflect the aspirations of a specific community. That week, we understood the basic principle of engaging community members in the workshop. It is their issue, not ours."

Once the community sets the framework that will guide its action, it can assess its current performance, as well as check on progress over time.

Community members grade the collective performance of each practice on a five-point scale, where level five describes the practice of the community when it has realized its dream. That is why we start with level five when we describe the performance of each practice.

For example, if the problem has been identified as brushing teeth, the practices are graded as follows.

5. We act in a natural way: "I feel dirty when I do not wash my teeth."
4. We act voluntarily and systematically: "I make the effort to brush my teeth morning and night, but sometimes my wife has to remind me."
3. We act sporadically: "I brush my teeth when I have time."
2. We know enough to act, but do not: "I know how to brush my teeth."
1. We are aware of the practice but do not know how to act: "I know I should brush my teeth."

If we apply this scale to the practice of inclusion of families affected by HIV, we may formulate something like this.

5. The affected family members participate fully in the life of our community.
4. We ensure the systematic inclusion of affected families in schools, workplaces, and markets, and during social events. We systematically deal with incidents of discrimination.
3. We act from time to time, but basically we discriminate.
2. We know how to include the affected families, but we do nothing.
1. We would like to include families affected, but how?

Once communities have adopted practices that will lead them to achieve their dreams, and once members have understood the levels of self-assessment, they are ready to assess current levels of practice. In this process, members reflect together and suggest a particular level for a particular practice while sharing their rationale for the assessment. Says the head of the Ugandan village on the road from Masaka to Rwanda, "For inclusion, it is clear. We are at level five. The world welcomes Uganda's progress against AIDS!"

However, the women laugh gently. "But, Chief, you know that we reject families with a patient in their midst! Not long ago, we told a Rwandan family to continue its journey because the husband was showing signs of the disease!"

A lengthy discussion ensues, others contribute opinions that often contradict each other, and the chief agrees to review the assessment. Finally, the members agree on level three and decide to invite a person from a community living with AIDS to the next town meeting. The discussion has given the community a better grasp of its situation. By building on this understanding, it will decide what actions to take in order to include infected people and their families as a natural part of their lives.

Sometimes the self-assessment can build a stronger sense of cohesion and create an opening to receive vital information from unexpected sources. In 2005, a team from a UN agency in Madagascar had completed the self-assessment of its AIDS competence. Everyone was present, from the security guard to the management. The team had started discussing ways in which they could reduce their risk of acquiring HIV when a senior staff members said, "We all know how dangerous our roads are. In our work, we have to constantly to travel by road. This means that can be injured in an accident and get transfused. However, we do not even know which hospitals test blood for HIV before it is transfused!"

A driver replied, "But we do know! Our UN drivers association maintains a list of hospitals that test blood for HIV before a transfusion."

Here is another example from a village in the Sikasso region of Mali. In separate groups, men and women have completed the self-assessment of their response to HIV, and they are now pooling the results. "In respect to gender relations, we are at level five," say the men.

"No," respond the women. "If a level zero existed, that is where we would rate our community." An animated public debate ensues. Unfortunately, I leave before the discussion ends, but I can bet that even if the men and women do not arrive at a consensus, there will be action!

We have noticed a trend in self-assessments. Men and senior staff tend to depict the situation in more general terms, and they give the community more generous scores. Women and field workers tend to be more practical and realistic in their assessments. When faced with these different viewpoints, the facilitator does not need to panic; he only needs to request that the disagreeing parties justify their positions. When the community considers the situation from different angles, it builds a stronger base for action.

The self-assessment can lead to many kinds of actions. First, there is the search for necessary information for action. "We hear about AIDS, but our knowledge is superficial." The "L" in SALT guides the facilitation team to link the community with a locally available source of information. "We want to stop discrimination in our neighbourhood, but how?" Again, the facilitation team links the community with another community that has solved the issue.

Then there is the use of prevention and care services and commodities. "We want to know our HIV status," say more than four hundred of the six hundred prisoners at Kananga in the DRC. "Now, we shall use condoms during our fishing trips," decide the fishermen in Mbandaka in the DRC. Once communities make these decisions, they put pressure on service providers to see that the resources required for the services are available in sufficient quantities. For example, after their self-assessment in Madagascar, a community from a remote province visited the head of the national AIDS programme to demand that the team screen the entire community for HIV. And it was done!

Finally, there are the many local actions that communities undertake without external support. For example, many communities all over the world contribute to support AIDS orphans. In northern Togo, women's clubs manage the local malaria program. In the Walis Station settlement of Mount Hagen in Papua, youths organize a weekly coffee night on Wednesdays, without alcohol or drugs. In Thailand, communities offer alternative livelihood for sex workers who return home because they lost their jobs after a positive HIV test.

Communities repeat the self-assessments every six months or every year, and they adjust their actions. The Ta Wang Tan community near Chiang Mai has been doing this exercise since 2004. Members will show you the results of successive self-assessments, explaining how their priorities have evolved. They will tell you how they started with the dream of reducing discrimination, invite you to visit the centre for young people, explain how they helped people living with HIV before antiretroviral drugs were available, and detail what they are doing to help discordant couples[1] to overcome their difficulties. Currently, they are working with the issue of HIV in the context of unintended pregnancies among adolescent girls.

In the next chapter, we will see how communities learn from each other to adapt their actions.

---

[1] Where one of them is infected and the other is not.

CHAPTER 11

Something to Learn, Something to Share

"Z'azis puis ze réflécis! I act first, and then I think!" Achille Van Acker, the Belgian politician, is remembered for these words, spoken with a heavy accent. At least he was reflecting! Like Van Acker, the Constellation is committed to the process of reflection after each major activity. We call this process After Action Review (AAR), or more recently, Reflection After Action (RAA). Facilitators compare their perspectives after each event——a community visit, a learning event, a meeting, and so on—— and ask themselves three questions.

- What went well, and why?
- What might be improved, and why?
- What did we learn for the next time?

One might think that the process is tedious. On the contrary, joint reflection that leads to action is an inexhaustible source of joy.

In 2004, Geoff and I visited the School of Public Health in Rio de Janeiro. During the preparation, I requested a faculty member organize a morning visit to a favela. The assistant accepted readily, and we met just behind the school. On our return, we held the AAR while standing on a street near the highway.

"I am very happy," the assistant who organized the visit said. "For the first time, visitors to the school have asked me to organize such a trip!"

"I, too, was glad to walk with you in the favela and visit all these NGOs that work for the well-being of its inhabitants," I replied. "But I was expecting to converse with the inhabitants rather than with the NGO leaders who do not live there."

"Why did you not ask to do that?" the assistant asked.

"Sorry for not being explicit, but this seemed the obvious thing to do," I replied.

The silence settled as we each thought about this exchange. Then we concluded that in future I would be more explicit in the way I formulated my requests, and the assistant would ask more questions to make sure she understood them.

When we work as a group for a few days, I love the particular moment when we reflect on the events of the previous day. Before resuming our work, we stand in a circle to share the thoughts that we might have had overnight or those that have come up when we regroup. The atmosphere is quiet, the pace is slow, and the space for sharing is created. The pastor in Port Moresby used that space the morning after his first SALT visit the previous day. "I have not slept all night. When my wife asked me why, I described yesterday's visit and explained how it had changed my outlook on people. Interested, she requested to join me and suggested we take our daughter with us. I am pleased to introduce them to you." On another occasion, Mike, a facilitator at RDC Compétence, shared during morning reflection, "That's it——now I understand. SALT is not a protocol; it is a way of life."

When we are faced with an unexpected event, we tend to act on the basis of our hypothesis about why it happened. But in order to learn, we must be ready to challenge all our certainties. This happens when we combine the different perspectives of the group on what took place. Here's a story to illustrate this point. It is 7.00 p.m. on June 20, 2011, the first day of a nationwide learning event on HIV and handicap. Rui Maquene Boëne drives us back to Maputo, where he works for Handicap International. After a journey of thirty kilometres, we stop at a red light on top of a hill. Team members chat in the rear of the car. Rui takes advantage of the halt to answer text messages on his cell phone. Night has fallen, and the screen of his phone casts a dim light on his face. He is focused on the task at hand: organizing community visits for one hundred participants the next day——not an easy task! While he writes, we feel a jolt at the back of our car. Rui stops writing and looks up, wondering who has hit us. I can see some anger on his face. "Take it easy," I say. "It is we who hit the car behind us, not the reverse. Our car pulled back a little as you were focused on your texting." Rui steps out and calmly greets the other driver. They do not notice any damage, and we leave in a good mood.

When members of the community express different perceptions of reality, facilitation creates the space for a conversation that brings everyone to a new understanding of their experience. The art of facilitation is to find the natural rhythm that will allow the group to discuss, reflect, and learn, in order to improve action. This rhythm is made of debates as well as of profound silence. At first, participants dread the moments of silence, and the facilitators have to enforce them. Gradually, group members create a greater sense of community as they come closer to perceiving their common reality.

But how do we proceed when several communities come together to learn from each other? We can distinguish two situations. The first is when a community visits another community to make progress on a specific practice. The second is when many communities share their experiences with life competence. We call the first process a peer assist, and the second a learning festival.

A peer assist is nothing more than a conversation designed to extract and adapt from the experience of others in resolving a specific challenge. For example, a community that wants to move towards the inclusion of sexual minorities might visit another community where these minorities live in harmony. During the peer assist, visitors begin by expressing their needs and the ideas they have to resolve the issue. The more specific their request, the greater their chances of getting answers. Next, the hosts ask questions to better understand and appreciate the situation of the visitors. Only after reflecting on this situation will the hosts provide suggestions based on their experience (rather than their opinion). Visitors listen with the serene attention necessary for resonance.

Here is an example of a learning festival. At the end of a series of community visits in northern Thailand, visitors and guests took part in a day-long learning festival. MariJo, Tew, Lawan, and I formed a group to share our experience about the inclusion of people living with HIV in the society. Tew is a health volunteer in Ta Wang Tan, and MariJo Vasquez is a writer in Barcelona. They have met for the first time, and they now want to further explore their experience of living with AIDS. Lawan serves as an interpreter. We sit in a circle on the floor, and Tew tells us how it started, what she went through, and how she gives her time and energy to visit families affected by AIDS. Although she is illiterate, she is accompanied by a young man who writes her report. MariJo chimes in with her experience as a woman living with AIDS in Europe. Both women reflect. Tew says, "Basically, it would have been easier if we had not been the object of so much attention. If I had to do it again, I would be careful not ask too much. I'd just request to be considered 'normal', no more, no less." MariJo adds, "This is my experience in Europe as well!" Lawan translates through her tears. Soon the emotion engulfs all four of us. The session ends, and we embrace each other. The conversation has produced a shared principle: "To include people living with HIV, do not give them special status, but consider them as normal people, no more or less."

If communities around the world had similar conversations where they relate their own experiences and validate such principles, wouldn't the process produce a new form of global wisdom born of collective experience? Here is another example. At a learning festival, the one where Rabindran decided to change his attitude towards homosexuals, our subgroup of about a dozen discussed the practice of reducing our vulnerability. A lady recounts her experience. "For many years, I have been running an NGO in Lampang, in northern Thailand. We train youth peer educators in the field of reproductive health. Jiew was a peer educator I liked a lot. I would call her a five-star educator! But she suddenly stopped showing up at our meetings——she was gone. Concerned about her fate, I made discreet enquiries. I soon learned that Jiew was pregnant, and a few weeks later, her problem was solved! When she finally returned to see me after several months of absence, I told her how sad I was, because I had so wanted to support her through her ordeal. Jiew answered, 'Mom, you always demanded perfection. I did not want to disappoint you.' Since that day, I decided that I would no longer demand perfection, but would help young people to learn from their mistakes." The lady fell silent, and the group began to reflect.

Then a Cambodian participant said, "I have a similar experience!" He told us a story about street children in Phnom Penh. From the sharing of experiences from Lampang and Phnom Penh, a common principle emerged: "Allow for mistakes so that people can learn from them." Other group members were asked to share their stories. Gradually we built a pearl of wisdom, which included common principles for action, the experiences that buttressed them, and the contact details of people from whom we could learn more.

Unlike a peer assist, a learning festival requires more complex skills. Participants should know how to succinctly recount their experience and distil the lessons they have learned from it. Next, they have to listen to appreciate the experience of others, detecting what resonates with their own. This attitude requires a change in the mode of listening, because most often people listen for difference: "Great what you did, but you come from a poor/rich/Catholic/Muslim country, and our situation is different." They then use that difference as a pretext for not learning from what is shared, and they avoid questioning their own ways. This is how global policymakers failed to learn from the experience of northern Thailand, and they dismissed it instead by citing sociocultural differences. Had they tried to seek principles for action in the experience, it could have inspired the formulation of global AIDS strategies, and it could have challenged the certainties of the international community.

We have seen that the combination of conversation, reflection, and action strengthens community practice. While the expert distinguishes specific issues such as AIDS, malaria, or domestic violence, humans are interested in a better life and therefore realize that their challenges are linked. So too are the solutions to those challenges. Isn't it natural that communities use the processes they have learnt to meet any challenge they encounter? Once facilitators see themselves primarily as human beings, they are inspired by the appreciation of community strengths, and they learn to envision their own relationships differently. This not only transforms people, it transforms organizations, as we will see in the following chapters.

CHAPTER 12

This Is about Life Competence!

Everything begins with a reflection on life. Indeed, to tackle AIDS, communities and families need to discuss and reflect on their way of life. Will men accompany their wives to antenatal screening for HIV, and why? Should community members promote premarital screening, and if yes, what would they do with the results? How do we keep young people out of prostitution while society seems to equate happiness with the acquisition of more and more goods? How do we help discordant couples? At what age should sex education begin, and who should take responsibility for it? How do we help people who work away from home for months, and what can we offer those who remain? Discussions about these issues are unavoidable, and they expose fundamental values, relationships, and roles within communities and families. In turn, communities do not limit their response to the use of inputs such as condoms, HIV tests, and antiretroviral drugs; they mobilize themselves to act on all fronts.

In Papua New Guinea, a community has addressed these questions and has started to take action. It is October 2008. The Wallis Station community reviews its progress since it adopted SALT a few months earlier. Eli, a youth leader, says that the focus on strengths has made him proud of his community, especially of young people acting to reduce their consumption of alcohol and drugs. They have organized weekly coffee nights where they discuss their hopes and concerns, including HIV, alcohol, and drug use. The youngsters screened a video on HIV borrowed from the Red Cross, and they raised the money for the gasoline for the generator, and for coffee for all those who attended. Someone lent his TV.

They have also cleaned up their neighbourhood and have invited youth from neighbouring communities to their coffee nights. According to their assessment, drug use has decreased by 70 per cent. A mother summarizes the progress: "Now we can sleep at night. Earlier, young people and drug addicts would keep us awake with their shouting and fighting! Not to mention gunshots or the screams of girls who were raped ... Since we took things in hand to respond to AIDS, we now sleep."

When a community meets the challenge of AIDS, it emerges stronger; in fact, it appears that nothing can stop it from achieving what it wants. Ban Pang Lao is on the road from Chiang Rai in northern Thailand, close to the famous Golden Triangle. Khun Sumalee, a tall woman with greying hair, teaches at the village school with her husband. She welcomes you into a small room full of light. Through the windows, you can see banana and mango trees and all the greenery of the garden. In the rainy season, tender green paddy fields stretch to the horizon. Khun Sumaleecan gives you a fascinating and detailed description of all the phases of the community response to AIDS. Yet now she directs her passion elsewhere. "Since we've been through this ordeal, we are ready to meet any challenge. For instance, young people have kept the village safe from drug dealers seeking to establish themselves here. The solidarity fund we created to help families affected by AIDS now serves all kinds of projects developed by and for the community." Returning to the topic of HIV, she describes a program implemented by the community for construction workers who leave for long months to take jobs in the Gulf area. All returned healthy.

The residents of the Manhay Centre, located in the heart of the Belgian Ardennes, have a similar experience. The centre, a former vacation home, now hosts political asylum seekers in Belgium. Within six months of a visit by a team of facilitators from BelCompetence in 2008, the residents formed a club, ManhayCompétence, with the goal of becoming AIDS competent and sharing their experience with newcomers. Aude, a BelCompétence facilitator, recounts how a participant tossed a condom into the middle of the circle, exclaiming, "I am aware that AIDS exists, and I always take care of myself. It's too important. Besides, I think we have no excuse. Here in Manhay, you know that we can have free condoms. Who else can say today that they are taking care of themselves?" Two other participants drew condoms from their pockets and waved them at everyone, effectively silencing those who had done most of the talking until then. What an awesome moment!

One participant had graded himself at level five during the self-assessment, and a group member asked, "Have you been tested for HIV since you came here? You say that you always have a condom on you, but what about the test?"

The man replied, "Yes! I have stayed in Manhay for ten months now, and I can tell you that I went for three tests! And I will keep going. If you want, I will show you my results."

Another expressed the feelings of many of the participants: "To move forward, I must be okay with myself and know that I am worth something. Otherwise, I have no value as a man. As I wait for a response to my asylum request, away from my country, what purpose do I serve? I have no family, I am not allowed to have a job, and I feel worthless."

Smiling at his recollections, Aude concludes, "So much was shared that day! Some told their life stories with such ease, and their sharing stimulated other group members to express their fears and their questions, and to contribute with their own experiences!"

In January 2009, the Manhay Centre was tasked with the creation of a new centre for asylum seekers in Beho, a small village near the Luxembourg and German borders. The landscape is cold and grim——a severe contrast for residents, most of whom come from tropical climates. Some Manhay residents had moved to Beho and they decided to transfer the SALT approach to a concern more pressing than AIDS. Yvette, who worked as an accountant at a Chinese construction company in Bujumbura and is an active member of BelCompétence after being granted asylum, said, "After participating in the learning festival organized by BelCompétence, we realized that we could change our lives ourselves by joining forces and relying on our experience to deal with life issues. During a conversation with visitors from BelCompétence, we raised the issue of our integration with the local Beho community. Some members had insulted us, insinuating that we were scoundrels and criminals. As part of pursuing our dream of an integrated Beho, we decided to host a world dinner at the centre. Our agenda for the evening: welcoming guests, interactions between visitors and residents, drinks, and dinner prepared by the Congolese, Guinea, and Afghan communities, followed by music. For the residents, many of whom were qualified as doctors, singers, electricians, mechanics, and so on, it was an opportunity to express themselves and to reveal their ability to contribute to society.

"At the next self-assessment, residents found that after that evening, relations between them and the local community had improved. Community members donated clothes and furniture, offered them a ride to the shopping mall, and invited them to religions functions. On their part, the residents helped to clean up the village and joined in summer vacation activities. African women even started hair braiding for the children in the neighbourhood! Preparing the world dinner event together had also united the residents. Previously, residents often had fights that would sometimes even damage equipment in the centre, and the Belgian Red Cross would transfer the troublemakers to other centres without addressing the causes of the conflicts. After the dinner, the fights stopped, and Beho started welcoming troublemakers from other centres."

Louis-Marie was a facilitator who accompanied the transition from Manhay to Beho, and from AIDS Competence to Life Competence. Also from Burundi, he knows the situation of asylum seekers and works with the Belgium Red Cross as a social worker. He recalls the transition. "Before we adopted the SALT approach, only a small group of residents was interested in training to build their capacities. But when they built their dream of inclusion, many more residents wanted to undergo training of all kinds. 'Let me use my time and skills to do something useful and not just receive,' was how they began to think. At the Red Cross, we were overwhelmed and unable to respond to all the applications for training. I suggested that the residents organize a skills fair within the centre itself, where different people could offer to teach their skills to others:——literacy, cooking, sewing, use of the Internet.——The residents themselves became teachers and learners, and some like Yvette are now facilitators in BelCompétence."

Louis-Marie concludes, "My own view of asylum seekers has also changed. Now, I consider them for who they are——human beings with strengths. The mere fact that they made it to Belgium is already proof of their strength!"

In these examples, communities built on their response to AIDS to progress towards life competence. But the process can also work in reverse.

Here is an example. One morning, a delegation from Bagamoyo District, Tanzania, paid a visit to Clement Cha Cha, at the Muhimbili Hospital at Dar es Salaam University. In Bagamoyo, communities have used the life competence process, transferred by Clement, a Constellation coach, to address malaria. The delegation had a request. "AIDS is a serious threat in our community. Now that we address malaria by ourselves, please help us adapt the malaria competence approach to strengthen our response to AIDS."

Other issues can also become entry points for communities to progress to life competence. In Togo it was malaria. Renowned for its health service, Togo took advantage of the national immunization day in 2004 to distribute impregnated bed nets to each family. Health authorities had organized an impeccable campaign which combined supply logistics with information, education, and communication. But the results were disappointing: only 37 per cent of families had used the nets!

Blaise Sedoh, the head of health at the Togolese Red Cross, was aware of the problem. This discreet, humorous man, with eyes sparkling behind large glasses that ate up his face, grasped the opportunity to apply the malaria competence approach. Blaise had earlier facilitated AIDS competence and had participated in a seminar in Mombasa on adapting the approach to malaria. He persuaded the Red Cross to try. A year later, bed net use had increased from 37 per cent to over 80 per cent in provinces where communities had managed the entire response. Because this was most often done by women, the Red Cross gave them a certificate to acknowledge their role. This was the first time that some of them had a document that bore their identity! The men were quick to admit the women's role. "We men handle problems in general terms. Our women go into detail. Since they took care of malaria in our community, no child has died during the rainy season."

Joked one woman, "When investigators used to ask us who slept under the net in our village, how could they be sure that we told them the truth? Now we can enter into houses and see for ourselves." The Togolese Red Cross, the Swiss Red Cross, and the University of Basel confirmed that communities that practiced malaria competence witnessed a significant reduction in mortality compared to those using the traditional approach. In Togo, one no longer speaks of malaria competent, but of life competent communities.

CHAPTER 13

Inspiration Flows

AIDS competence spreads faster than the virus. That was our vision when we founded the Constellation, and it's happening! Once people realize their own potential, and that of their community, they stand up and share that realization with others, who in turn gain the confidence to share their own experiences. The phenomenon goes viral. Realizing one's own strengths and of those of others triggers a different kind of epidemic:——a positive one.

Gabriel Ringlet, former vice-rector of the Catholic University of Louvain, defines spirituality as the flow of energy, and he compares a spiritual person to a priest who is destined to transfer a huge amount of energy! After years of reluctance, I now acknowledge a spiritual dimension to our work at the Constellation, although I did not anticipate it, much less plan for it. I have to admit that appreciating the strengths of communities allows facilitators to channel energy for transformation.

Merauke in Papua province is a hot spot for AIDS in Indonesia. It borders Papua New Guinea, and getting there feels like travelling to the end of the world. After an overnight flight from Jakarta and a stopover at Jayapura, the capital of Papua, we fly south for an hour before landing in a vast plain at the edge of the Pacific Ocean. Here, many years ago, the indigenous Melanesian residents were joined by Papuans from the high mountains and by Javanese, who settled in with the help of a national transmigration program aimed at alleviating overcrowding.

The members in our group have come from Jakarta, Australia, and Belgium to meet the local facilitation team in Merauke. HIV incidence had increased exponentially, and the reports of experts suggested a growing weariness with their efforts to address the problem. It was our third visit, and we were certain of one thing at least:——the changes we saw in people had transformed members in the facilitation team as well.

Ian is a leader of a rock band. This handsome young man talks about how music is often accompanied by alcohol, drugs, and girls. He says that his engagement with the community helped him decide to stop drinking and focus on his music. Other members in the band have decided to follow suit.

Ibu Winona tells us how her sex life has improved after listening to a sex worker whom she befriended during successive visits to a karaoke bar, and how she has shared her experiences with local women in her own community.

Ibu Henny is an assistant to the mayor. A lawyer by training, she has repeatedly been confronted with cases of domestic violence in her own community. "Each time, I used to think, Why do these women let themselves be beaten up by their husbands? Why are these women so weak? Now I listen without judging. I appreciate the strengths of the women. How can they change if I do not change the way I look at them?"

Dany, one of the Papuans who came from the high mountains, is a pastor. Despite his massive girth and strong features, I sense a gentle and peaceful person. He is used to speaking, and when he speaks, people listen. Dany tells us how his visits to communities in Merauke made him think of his own. "Many things happen in my community that make us vulnerable. Since becoming part of this team, I felt I had to warn my people."

The changes are not limited to members of the local facilitation team. Visitors also have changed.

Matt Campbell has joined us for the first time in Merauke. The Australian may be the youngest person in our group, but he has the most experience with community visits, having done hundreds. "In Merauke, I was reminded of my personal journey towards life competence. Appreciation has transformed me. I've changed, and I found a new hope in my life because some people chose to focus on what I could do, not on what I could not. By focusing on what was possible, I was able to face what seemed impossible."

Harry is a leader in the gay community in Indonesia. He is an outstanding facilitator, full of intelligence and humour. "I learned a lot from the people of Merauke. They showed me the love of life and proved that people can use their own forces to respond to AIDS. Each of their life stories touched me personally. I returned to Jakarta with a smile and a thought: 'Why always discuss problems and negative aspects while the strengths and positive things can be the source of change?'" That is what he set out to practice in his organization, PKKBI (Praktik Kewarganegaraan Kami Bangsa Indonesia, or Practice of Citizenship in the Indonesian Nation), a well-known national NGO in the field of reproductive health.

Rysia is a third-time visitor. "We knew Ibu Yosefa as a timid woman who spoke only when someone asked her to lead a prayer. I could not believe my eyes when I saw her demonstrate the use of the female condom in front of thirty people with a naughty look on her face. From being so shy, she is so full of confidence now! Her demonstration inspired me and others. Love, understanding, and concern for others changes not only individuals but also those around them." Rysia had later gone on to facilitate a community's dream in Sulawesi, and this led to the ousting of its corrupt mayor.

In our experience, the process of appreciating strengths makes us stronger, and we pass them on. Phil Forth is part of the support team of the Constellation. He left his position as a senior manager at BP to become an independent consultant in knowledge management. He values the contribution of the Constellation's positive approach to his private practice, and he gives 50 per cent of his time to help the Constellation summarize its learning from the ground, and to continuously adapt its approach to communities. Speaking to a group of visitors to a community in northern Thailand who had expressed a concern that they were not giving anything tangible to their hosts, Phil says, "I have told this story twice within the Constellation, and on each occasion I have felt a little embarrassed and uncomfortable. But what happened was so powerful for me and changed what I do so dramatically that I thought I would share it here.

"My wife was a governor at our local secondary school. It is quite large, about 1,400 pupils. Well, as sometimes happens, there was a struggle between an old set of governors who believed they knew best how to run the school and a new head teacher. This led to conflict within the school's governing body. My wife took supported the new head. Initially, she was on her own and had to battle long and hard. There were a lot of nervous evenings, both before and after confrontations, and at one stage, she even feared there would be physical violence. As you can imagine, all this involved many late nights, and I did my best to support and encourage her. But one day, at the end of a very long evening, I said, 'What you are doing is a good thing. You are a good person for doing this, and you must be proud of yourself. The education of lots and lots of children will improve because of what you are doing.' I'm not sure if I realized at the time that I had moved from supporting her to appreciating her. And her response? She was annoyed! She said I was talking nonsense and that she was only doing the right thing, nothing more. So I left it at that. Perhaps there was a time to appreciate and a time to keep quiet.

"Time went by. Then quite suddenly, my wife died. One Friday she was working at another school, and on the following Monday she was dead! Her job had been to arrange support for children who had special educational needs. This could range from helping children who lived their short lives in a wheelchair to arranging extra help for a sixteen-year old who had trouble reading and writing. After her death, there was a flood of letters from many people. And time after time, the letters from her colleagues said how my wife had told them that the work that they were doing was a good thing, that they must be proud of what they were doing, and that their work would change the life of a human being. They wrote that what my wife had said had inspired them in their efforts, and they had in turn passed on the message to a colleague! I haven't the slightest idea how far the message has spread, but I suspect that one act of appreciation several years ago is still influencing people in my part of the world, and that gives me a quiet satisfaction."

Phil's summarizes two key elements in the transformation of a facilitator. Facilitators are primarily driven by the energy generated by communities whose strengths they have appreciated. In turn, they transfer the energy to effect change in their own context. Thus, Phil was doing something unusual in his culture when he appreciated his wife's work—— but then, in which culture do spouses easily express the strengths they see in each other? Plus, it changed her own response to her colleagues.

Phil's story still influences people, and not only in his part of the world. Abednego Mutungwa, a Kenyan coach, decided to examine how to spell out the specific strengths we discern in our own families. "How do those who are dear to us discover their own strength? I decided to try the approach with my wife. At dinner one day, in the presence of my two sons, I said to her, 'My dear, you have a gift for creating beautiful things!'

"'Why do you say that?' she asked.

"'Just look at our garden. What a wonderful combination of flowers you have created! And look at the beautiful beads you made of recycled paper at Dorcus Beads.'

"My wife replied that although I was not the first one to appreciate her work, it made her very happy. I decided that from now on, when we discussed joint projects with the family, the best way was to build on our strengths rather than trying to judge each other."

The first time I realized that facilitators were also affected by the process of appreciating strengths was in May 2006 in Lemba, a municipality in Kinshasa. The core facilitators of the Congolese RDCCompétence were meeting three months after their initial training. I asked what they had learnt since the training, expecting a comment on their experience of using some of the tools we had offered as part of the training process. But without exception, everybody described changes in their own behaviour. This is what Antoine said about the changes in his family.

"On December 1 last year, I came back home after working as a consultant at the UNAIDS office. During dinner, I showed my family two large posters designed for the World AIDS Say. The posters featured portraits of women with the words, 'When will you listen to me?'

"When I went to bed, a surprise awaited me. Someone had stuck one of the posters on the door to the bedroom! I turned around to see the other poster pinned on the door to the girls' bedroom. 'What's going on?' I asked, taken aback.

"'Dad, you know that you never have time for us. And nothing we do is good enough for you!'

"I looked at my wife. She said, 'This is the World AIDS campaign, is it not?' I did not sleep too well that night and slowly forgot the incident.

"A few weeks later, I was returning from Kimbanseke, after appreciating the strengths of a very poor community. As we were driving back downtown

Kinshasa I thought to myself, What if I tried this at home? So I started to compliment my wife on the meals she prepared, and I congratulated my daughters on their achievements at school. One day I noticed that the posters had disappeared. I asked my wife and the girls, 'Why did you remove the posters?'

"My wife replied, 'You know very well why I took them down. You have changed!'

But the girls protested, 'No, Mom, you should not have removed the posters. You did not change!'"

In October 2010, about sixty participants in the International SALT Visit at Koppal in Karnataka, India, as well as members of the communities they had visited, gathered for half a day of reflection and sharing. I was to facilitate the meeting and was a little anxious. In the preceding three days, teams of participants had each visited six communities and had a lot to share. What format should I offer to make this time as profitable as possible for everybody?

The meeting room we had booked in the hotel was not available, so we met in the garden. While sitting under the beautiful trees, the teams reviewed all that they had learned. Once in a while, the rumble of a passing train intruded upon our lively conversations. Suddenly my attention was caught by a truck that entered the hotel garden with a full load of tall bamboos and yards of colourful fabric. Soon after, workers requested we move as they busied themselves in raising a bright yellow hall, using the bamboos as stilts and the cloth as the covering. My anxiety peaked. "Oh, my God. The hotel has organized a traditional wedding on today of all days! Where in the world are we going to meet now?"

Almost immediately, a friend from Samraksha, the host organization, reassured me. The beautiful room was meant for us, for our learning festival! While the sixty people took their seats, I told myself, "Next time I'll follow the advice posted in my office: 'Are you sure?'"

Soon, the participants were ready to resume. Joao, from Mozambique, stood in the middle of the hall and told us how he'd listened to a man who had lost his brother to AIDS, despite the good care the man had given. Joao said that the story had resonated with him, and he had shared that his sister was living with AIDS. "Yes," the man replied, "but your sister is still alive, and you can always take care of her. As for me, my brother is gone, and there is nothing I can do for him anymore!"

"His reply struck me," said Joao. "I have worked for ten years against AIDS in my country, but what have I done for my sister? Just before I left for this trip, she asked me to buy a hair dryer to equip the salon she wants to open. And what did I do? I spent all my money shopping for myself! So I called my sister from Koppal to ask her for forgiveness. She told me that she always knew that I would come to her one day, 'Because you're a good man!' I told her to buy the hair dryer right away, and I would reimburse her on my return." Joao finished his story and returned to his seat in tears. The silence was profound. The participants were engrossed in their thoughts, and some were crying. I cannot read minds, but that day I sensed that many of us thought about our own family histories. Through Joao, the story of a man who lost the brother he loved resonated with all of us.

After giving everyone time to recover, I said, "Joao, your story says it all. You listened deeply, the story has changed you, and you transferred your experience in your own context."

Joao's story inspired Sanghamitra, the head of Samraksha, to call her mother. "It's Diwali next week, our biggest festival in India," she told me. "Usually I do not fly to Delhi to see my mother and the rest of my family for Diwali, because I keep thinking that I'm too busy. But I have told her that this time I will join the celebrations. My mother was surprised and asked, 'Why do you want to come? I'm not sick; there is no need for you to visit!' I replied, 'Wouldn't be great to meet while we are both well?'"

The following weekend, I travelled with Sanghamitra through the beautiful North Karnataka region, where we met with other communities and staff members of Samraksha. Those who had participated in the learning festival in Koppal recalled Joao's story and said how they had decided to practice appreciating strengths in their own context. In a chain reaction, others said, "I'll try this at home. I'll try this in my community."

A chain reaction! This is how we interpret the incredible numbers in the DRC, where in 8 months, 622 communities were able to show progress against HIV instead of the expected 225. In Mbuji Mayi, the capital of Kasai Oriental, a support team of 3 people trained 44 facilitators from 20 communities to facilitate the development of AIDS competence. Determined to share the approach with more communities beyond their own, they did not stop there. Six months later, these communities were sharing the approach with a third set of communities, leading to a total of 120 communities influenced by the approach, rather than the 20 originally planned.

The phenomenon is not new. Claire Campbell, the daughter of Ian, and Matt's sister, has documented the transfer of the approach from community to community in Zambia, India, and Bangladesh. From these experiences, one can estimate that when facilitators stimulate and accompany one community's response to a health or social challenge, members of that community will share the approach with three to four communities, thus influencing change in the whole entity.

We have only touched the surface of the spiritual dimension of the Constellation. At the end of 2010, Laurence and I invited Deng and Lawan to lunch. Deng is a leader among Thai people living with AIDS. I had first met Deng in *DoiSaket* in Chiang Mai in 1995, and he had made a strong impression. At his small centre next to the hospital, he and his now deceased wife began to offer advice and emotional support to people who came to learn about their HIV-positive status. Patients did not have access to antiretroviral treatment at the time, and their future was bleak, but Deng was able to explain his dream of a harmonious society. Since that time, we had met regularly.

On this occasion, Laurence and I wanted to explore with Deng why he was a Christian in a region with a strong Buddhist culture, whereas Laurence and I, both educated as Christians, were attracted by Buddhist practice. Very early into the conversation, we realized that the reasons were similar:——we wanted a practice that was free of the weight of institutional dogma. Later in the conversation, Deng spontaneously used SALT with a sparkle in his eyes, and we waited for Lawan to translate. "For Deng, SALT is the way to practice his religion."

Deng is also the secretary of the Thai Interfaith Network against AIDS (INAT), which adopted SALT as its way of working. He elaborated, "In fact, whether Christians, Buddhists, or Muslims, we all have the same experience. We find references in support of SALT in our respective teachings." A chapter in their manual details these references. Since then, different networks have restructured their visits to the homes of people affected by AIDS. Rather than plan the visit according to the religious affiliation of the family, they have organized them on a geographical basis. "After all," they said, "our approach is the same!"

Through SALT, both the subjects and the objects of appreciation are transformed. A positive energy flows through them and spreads rapidly to transform more people. Christians, Muslims, and Buddhists recognize this process as "theirs". How is the Constellation organized to support rather than constrain the free flow of inspiration? And will the inspiration be powerful enough to transform organizations? We discuss these questions in the next chapter.

CHAPTER 14

Spider or Starfish?

"How many lives does the Constellation influence?" my father asked me at dinner not long ago. I mumbled some figure, but the question kept me awake that night. We could count the thousands of trained facilitators around the world, and the people who downloaded tools from our website and began work, and the ones who had been inspired by other communities who had adopted the approach, and the many more who had heard us at meetings, seminars, and conferences. I realized that the Constellation had expanded to include more than a million people who acted locally in response to different issues: AIDS, malaria, diabetes, neighbourhood peace, the future of the planet. We will probably never know the exact figure, but does it really matter?

How did we support the rapid expansion of the Constellation? Since 2005, the Constellation global support team has been inviting ten to twenty people to Chiang Mai every year. We spend several days appreciating the strength of communities in this region, and then a day or two reflecting on what we have learnt and how we can apply it in our respective contexts. In September 2008, Amber, a journalist who worked with an NGO in Chiang Mai, was one of the visitors. Towards the end of the discussion, she said, "The clearest illustration of your approach is how you function. Everything went like clockwork, and yet we do not even know how you are organized. All of you are there for us, and we could not sense the slightest difference between you. We can't figure out a hierarchy, and no one even knows who the team leader is——but it does not matter! That's what I'm going to transfer to my own work." We were both flattered and surprised.

So far we had considered SALT as a way to facilitate local responses, but we did not realize that it applied within our own team!

Ian arrived for a whirlwind visit, as usual. Like a bee skipping from flower to flower, Ian pollinates our processes of reflection. Now he said, "SALT is the DNA of the Constellation." His statement has stuck.

We have been inspired by the world of the living organisms in organizing the global support team. In the living world, function creates form. Organs develop to support functions, not the other way around. Where functions are not needed, forms may atrophy but continue to consume resources. We decided to create the minimum number of structures that would be required to support the process of community life competence worldwide. Rather than seeking blueprints elsewhere, we decided to start afresh and build from the functions of the global support team team's support functions.

In 2006, we defined the functions of the support team as follows.

(i) Develop and maintain our approach for community life competence.

(ii) Transfer the approach to interested communities and networks.

(iii) Inspire communities to work towards life competence, and help them to connect for learning and sharing.

Phil wanted to know what the DNA and the processes were. He had created his own knowledge management firm and helped private companies organize real-time sharing of industrial process improvements globally. Attracted by our appreciative approach, he had decided to give 50 per cent of his time to the Constellation, and he has focused on understanding and formulating the essence of our approach. He systematically collects feedback as we acquire new insights from practice, and he helps us to evolve towards greater depth and simplicity. These insights are shared online. We call this function "Learn", although it can also be called "Adapt" because every organization needs to adapt to changes in its environment in order to survive.

Then we have "Transfer". Gaston, whom we met in chapter six, has coordinated this function out of Chiang Mai, followed by Olivia from London; currently, Laurie from France is holding the fort. Basically, this function consists of responding to communities that aspire to progress towards life competence. By community we mean any group of people who want to address a common concern. They may share a neighbourhood, a workplace, a faith, a disease condition, a social characteristic, and so on. In 2005, the Aga Khan Foundation was the first to invite us to transfer our approach to make their communities AIDS competent. We proposed to address the issue within their network of madrasas, hospitals, schools, and private companies, and we started training facilitators in the Aga Khan Development Network in Mombasa. Soon other communities, networks, businesses, and development agencies invited us to address a range of concerns, and we helped them recognize and strengthen their own capacity to formulate a collective vision, act on it, review progress, and adapt their actions to achieve it. We have since worked with eighty-six partnerships with fifty-one different partners in sixty-three different countries to support local responses and to develop life competence. Because we sell our services rather than ask for donor support, we can have greater control over the essence of our approach, and we test its relevance directly with communities in the field. In some cases, these communities do benefit from the support of an external agency, but they have the final say in deciding whether they want to work with us. For one to two years, Constellation coaches work alongside facilitators from within communities, practicing together in the field and learning together with guidance from our distance learning course.

The global support team is paid for from the difference between our fees and our costs. Our first contract with the Aga Khan Foundation helped to pay the team for three months, and our cash flow situation remains more or less the same. It is thus unlikely that our secretariat will burgeon into a bureaucracy! The approach has its limitations. First, payment of team members depends on new assignments and timely execution. This can tempt us into taking shortcuts to save money and quality. Sometimes it's potential partners, especially NGOs, who are accustomed to subsidies are reluctant because we sell our services. Others do not have the means to pay us. In such cases, we may offer our services for free, but travel costs can be very high, and we need to build a reserve fund to cope with these hazards. Fortunately, the majority of transfers takes place spontaneously from community to community, and it does not require formal intervention by Constellation facilitators!

This brings us to "Share", the third function of our support team. This function is also inspired by life. For example, bodies evolved from single-celled organisms, which began to communicate with each other and gradually formed a single body, served by a common nervous system. Similarly, the support team facilitates the communication between communities in order to facilitate mutual support and the emergence of a common understanding based on their various experiences. The online exchange platform on Ning performs this function. Initially hosted from Chiang Mai by Laurence, it is now hosted by Rituu B Nanda from New Delhi. The job involves sharing the inspiration and experience from communities, supporting people in the field with information and linkages, and (wherever possible) arranging face-to-face meetings to generate common knowledge. So far, over 1900 members from 96 countries are members of the platform. Although a lot more can be done to help practitioners fearlessly share their experiences with people from around the world, it is a pleasure to see facilitators from Guyana share experiences of life competence training for their country's police with their peers in Cambodia. These exchanges will gradually build into a goldmine!

Much remains to be done to identify common principles that emerge from the experiences of local responses, and to give them a wide circulation. Imagine the power of a constantly repeated process, leading people lead to continuously refine principles for action based on new experiences and in diverse settings! This would allow a constant flow of knowledge from local responses, available to players on the ground as well as to decision makers. We envision the development of a global organism composed of communities striving for life competence, driven by the energy released by local responses, led by common wisdom, and supported by the minimum organizational structure required for expanding and sustaining life competence.

While building the "Share" function, we had to be careful to remain focused on our core values. For example, we were repeatedly advised to segment the market, which meant that we should develop different messages for the different sectors that we interacted with——governments, associations, businesses, and so on. We resisted this advice because we believe that we interact with human beings, not with their business cards. They have strengths, weaknesses, hopes, and concerns independent of their professions, job responsibilities, areas of work, religions, or cultures. We believe that our language must be simple enough to appeal to the human being within all of us——the CEO, the homeless, the asylum seeker, the transsexual person, the priest, the prostitute, the police, the imam, the Buddhist monk, the minister, the nurse, their spouses, and their children.

We are able to hold on to our values because we make a conscious effort to unlearn our ways of being the expert, and to learn to behave as "normal" human beings. Along with a board of directors, Marlou coordinates overall support from her home in France. We call her function "Care" because care for the person is what keeps the functions together. On the day the exchange platform was launched, she wrote, "Many of you know that for many years, I have worked from my kitchen. I would put my laptop on the table and combine my role as a mother of four children with my work for the Constellation. My friends ask me if I don't feel lonely, all alone with my computer. But I smile, because I know how connected I feel with so many people in the world while just sitting at the table. This is where I learned from many of you while the soup warmed on the stove behind me, or the kids played with their Playmobil. We have shared laughter and tears——me at my table, you in your place. Some of you came to join me at the table for 'real' meetings, and I appreciate the moments when I can visit you in your own environments. These moments are precious because they make our virtual contacts all the more productive. Well, let me now return to my pans."

The global support team does not have a salary scale. Our aim is to ensure that all those working in the secretariat receive as much as they need to ensure similar standards of living, including access to good schools for children, to quality health services, and to a plan for retirement. We believe that facilitating local responses is an inborn skill, and thus anyone on the team can train to become one. This is how Lawan, our administrative assistant since 2005, became a Constellation coach. The same principle applies to the sixty coaches we have. When we work on a contract, we all are paid two hundred euros per day; the rest goes to the organization. Some of our best facilitators have not attended university but have stimulated real progress in their country. Take Onesmus, for example. From Kenya, Onesmus is the eldest of eight orphans, and he devoted himself to the education of his brothers and sisters. He did not have the opportunity to go to college, but his personal experience of life competence persuaded national leaders to adopt AIDS competence as a goal of its strategic plan.

When the number of facilitators in different countries began to grow rapidly, we needed to organize ourselves in these countries. Should we open subsidiaries, branches, divisions, or affiliates? Our Congolese friends resisted. "Affiliates? That word stems from the Latin *filius*, or son. A son implies a father and probably a subordinate relationship." So we opted for an egalitarian model. Member organizations serve facilitators within the country, and in turn, they are served by the global support team. There are currently twelve member organizations, with others in the making. Their functions are identical to those of the global support team, and they have the same structure. Each organization responds autonomously to invitations from the country and appeals to the global support team when cross-country exchanges are planned, or if the support of coaches from other countries is necessary. The persons performing learn, transfer, and share functions in each member organization, teaming up with peers who fulfil the same function anywhere in the world. It was only after we had established this model that Gaston discovered what we are: a starfish organization! What happens when the starfish loses a limb? It grows another, and a new starfish begins to grow from the isolated limb. This is possible because the intelligence of the starfish is diffused through every branch. Similarly, even if the Constellation implements different functions, our common understanding is so strong that each of us can form a new organization. This is in contrast to the spider model followed by many organizations:——if a leg is removed from a spider, it will not regrow, and the leg cannot grow itself into a new spider. If you cut off the head, that's the end of the spider. Luckily, the starfish has no head!

One evening before leaving to return to Kinshasa from Belgium, facilitators took turns to tell me what they had enjoyed during my visit, and I did the same for each of them. We call this time "watering the flowers". Mamy, a member of the board of directors of RDCCompétence, spoke last. "Jean-Louis, you may die, but we will continue to spread life competence!" Obviously that is a nice statement, but there is a long way to go! Even if life competence gradually spreads in neighbourhoods, businesses, and associations, how can progress be sustained while the public sector treats citizens as beneficiaries, and the private sector treats them as consumers? Our dream of global life competence can only be achieved if all stakeholders in public and private sectors build their own dream for the society of the future and rely on their collective intelligence and energy to realize it.

Policy support for life competence is possible. Consider UN organizations. The UNFPA in Indonesia, and the UNAIDS in Europe and Guyana, have adopted the appreciative approach in their programs. This has been possible because of the vision and cooperation of local officials who have been able to resist the dominant culture within these organizations. When they are replaced, progress within the organization can be threatened. Thus we need to target the culture within the organizations. To this end, the Constellation has concluded a formal cooperation agreement with UNAIDS and maintains excellent relations with its officials, including with Michel Sidibé, executive director since 2008. However, as long as the UN is primarily accountable to donors, its leaders are unlikely to be able to effect radical change. The system has to be reformed from inside out and top to bottom, and global citizens need to build their own vision of the UN. Only direct, democratic control of UN institutions can provide a counterweight to the power of donors.

Will private companies who want to better integrate social responsibility into their core business adopt a life competence approach? Only the future will tell. We have only just begun to invite private companies to join the movement. Christopher Boeraeve describes the effects of the approach on his law firm. "Our decisions have become more collegial. We found strength in our team that we did not know existed, and each member——assistants, junior, and senior lawyers——felt empowered. We have developed respect for the ability of each person to find solutions to the challenges facing us without renouncing authority and procedures. We have not yet achieved our dreams, but when our old habits tend to take over, we need to ask ourselves the question: What can I appreciate in our firm? In our strengths, we have a powerful antidote against the stupidity, wickedness, and selfishness that prevail in our industry.

CONCLUSION

There Is Another Way

No, Mr Fukuyama, this is not the end of history. The society in which we live is the not best possible one. The political, economic, financial, and even religious spheres have gradually drifted away from real life into a virtual reality where the only mantra is money. Meanwhile, the relentless noise of advertising, the continuous communication about disasters, and the antics of a few people tend to engage our individual and collective attention. We are witness the transformation of the world into a gigantic supermarket whose only purpose is to consume.

But we do not have to accept being reduced to the role of consumers! There is hope, tangible within and around us. We don't have to wait for a political or a religious redeemer who will save us from disaster. We can awaken and release our energy for change and transmit it to others, so that they in turn can regain the confidence to act towards recreating a better society.

How might this happen? Simply by changing our outlook! That takes only a fraction of a second. As we close this book, we can decide to tell persons close to us what we appreciate in them. This is easy enough to do with those whom we hold in high esteem. But to enjoy each other's strengths consistently in all situations, and with every person, is harder. If we are not careful, old habits will reassert themselves, and we will resume our inclination to judge, analyse shortcomings, and nourish our anger about what others don't do for us.

A change in outlook requires practice and discipline. Within the Constellation, we practice in teams with other communities. This helps to avoid "waking the old man who sleeps in us" when confronted with any difficulty. Let's face it: the older and the most educated among us, those who "have succeeded in life". will be tempted to unconsciously adopt reflexes acquired in other contexts. If we arm ourselves with healthy and constructive scepticism about our own experiences, consider the perspectives of others to better understand reality, and grasp the strengths that might have escaped our attention, this may inspire us. Let us practice appreciation of other communities, because it is from the relationship between communities that the energy for change will spring, both for the communities we visit and for our own.

Perhaps this way of seeing the world and of acting accordingly is already familiar to you. Indeed, the Constellation has invented nothing. We have developed an approach to meet an immediate challenge: to facilitate and link local responses to AIDS. That is our history. But we share our spiritual and philosophical heritage with other organizations and with other movements. If you belong to one of them, we invite you to unite forces to learn from each other and build on expertise born of common experiences. Let us join our voices to ensure that the principles born from local responses can serve to build the society of tomorrow.

Above all, let us act. No intellectual exercise, no theoretical model, no tool will replace the practice of appreciation. The community life competence process is simple, and its scope is wide and varied. Every human community can use it to cope with a common challenge, or to explore the deeper meaning of its actions.

It is up to you to decide what concern motivates you most. Do you want to rebuild a sense of community in your area? Are you part of an association of sick or disabled persons? Are you committed to health and welfare? Do you want to ensure that your business effectively contributes to a better society? Do you want to engage in political action beyond party politics? Build your team and go ahead with it. If you wish, download tools that might assist you from our website. And contact us if you want Constellation facilitators to work with you.

Let us control our destiny. As Hakim suggested, let us declare, loud and clear, our own right to dream. Let us unite with our loved ones to develop our dream, and let's rely primarily on our own resources to act and share with others the inspiration generated by our journey towards our vision.

Back in Koppal, North Karnataka, where Joao shared his experience under the beautiful yellow tent, our review of our experience with SALT is nearing completion. Another train passes nearby, and the rumble of its passage combines with a thunderous honking. Silence sets in. Lawan, our administrative assistant turned coach, gives the last statement. "There is another word whose first letter is included in SALT. That word is love."

AFTERWORD

And Now, What Can I Do?

After reading this book, are you interested to learn more about the Constellation?

Please visit our website: *www.communitylifecompetence.org*

Would you like to become a facilitator? Or would you like to get support from the Constellation to participate in the development of the community life competence of your specific community?

Please contact Marlou De Rouw at *marlou@communitylifecompetence.org*

Would you like to join us in our social network to share your experience?

We would be happy to hear from you at *www.aidscompetence.ning.com*

Would you like to make a donation to the Constellation to support communities in their actions?

Please make your contribution at the ABSL Constellation's donation account. IBAN BE62001579049761. Contributions in excess of 40 EUR are tax deductible in Belgium and some other European countries.

REFERENCES

Collison, C., Parcell, G. *Learning to Fly*, second edition. Capstone, 2005.

CDC. "Distribution of Insecticide-Treated Bednets during an Integrated Nationwide Immunization Campaign, Togo, West Africa, December 2004". *Morbidity and Mortality Weekly Report* 54 (39): 994–996. http://www.cdc.gov/mmwr/preview/mmwrhtml/mm5439a6.htm.

Duongsaa, U., et al. "Project of Participatory Learning from Local Responses in Northern Thailand". Unpublished report.

Forth, P. "The Power of Appreciation in SALT". Online Community of The Constellation, 2010. http://aidscompetence.ning.com/profiles/blogs/the-power-ofappreciation-

Forth, P. "AIDS Competence: How AIDS Competence Is Becoming a Reality through the Tools of Self-Assessment and Facilitation". UNAIDS, UNITAR, BP, The Salvation Army, 2004.

Gillot, L. and PNG Competence. "Papua New Guinea: Their Pride, Their Passion, Their Story". Video. Online Community of the Constellation, 2008. http://aidscompetence.ning.com/video/papua-new-guinea-their-pride.

Gillot, L., and PNG Competence. "My Life Is More Important". Online Community of the Constellation, 2008. http://aidscompetence.ning.com/video/my-life-is-moreimportant.

Kori, R. "The Strength Starts from There: How SALT Could Be so Powerful!" Online Community of the Constellation, 2010. http://aidscompetence.ning.com/profiles/blogs/ the-strength-starts-from.

Krishnamurti, J. *Freedom from the Known*. London: Harper One, 2009.

Lucas, S. "Community, Care Change and Hope: Local Responses to HIV in Zambia". The Synergy Project, 2004.

Nkurikiye, J. « n Intellectuel Retourné: Je Deviens l'Elève des Professionnelles du Sexe à Dar-es-Salaam ». Online Community of the Constellation, 2009. http:// aidscompetence.ning.com/profiles/ blogs/un-intellectuel-retourne-je.

Piot, P. "AIDS: From Crisis Management to Sustained Strategic Response". *Lancet* 368 (2006): 526–530.

Rumi, J. *The Essential Rumi*. C. Barks, trans. New York: Harper Collins Publishers, 2004.

Schmitz, G. "How My Dutch Experience Ends up in a Papua New Guinea Knowledge Asset". Online Community of the Constellation, 2008. http://aidscompetence.ning.com/ profiles/blogs/ how-my-dutch-experience-ends.

Schmitz, G. "What Is the Purpose of NGO Branding in the Field?" Online Community of the Constellation, 2010. http://aidscompetence.ning. com/profiles/blogs/what-is-thepurpose-of-ngo.

UNAIDS. HIV and Health Care Reform in Phayao: From Crisis to Opportunity. Best Practice Collection, Geneva, 2000. http://www. hivpolicy.org/Library/HPP000701.pdf.

WHO and UNAIDS. "Treating 3 Million by 2005: Making It happen". Geneva, The WHO Strategy, 2003. http://www.who.int/3by5/ publications/documents/isbn9241591129/en.

WHO and UNAIDS. "Progress on Global Access to HIV Antiretroviral Therapy: A Report on "3 by 5" and Beyond". Geneva, 2006. http:// www.who.int/hiv/progreport2006_en.pdf.

World Bank and UNAIDS. "Seminar on Responding to the HIV/AIDS Crisis: Lessons from Global Best practices: Sharing Ideas from Brazil, Senegal, Thailand, and Uganda". 2004. http://documents.worldbank. org/curated/en/2004/06/7036943/joint-world-bank-unaidsseminar-responding-hivaids-crisis-lessons-global-best-practices-sharing-ideas-brazilsenegal-thailand-uganda.

ENDORSEMENTS

"Jean-Louis Lamboray is one of the world's most impressive public health doctors. He has organized and led highly successful and creative campaigns against the AIDS virus, and managed systematic reform of the health system in Zaire (DR Congo). Lamboray's ideas are original and brilliant, and they've worked in practice. In *What Makes Us Human?* Lamboray explores the human connections that join us together, and the ways in which all individuals, working locally, can create a better world for themselves and us all without reliance on hierarchies of authority imposed from above."

– Richard Preston, contributor to *The New Yorker*, currently working on a successor book to *The Hot Zone*.

"Trust makes ordinary people do extraordinary things."
– Frédéric Laloux, author of the bestseller *Reinventing Organisations*

"Jean-Louis's stories make the reader pause to reflect about practical ways to address a wide range of life concerns. At the Ministry of Health of Senegal, we try very hard to stimulate community ownership of health issues. His book will help us take further action."

– Awa-Marie Coll-Seck, Minister of Health and Social Affairs, Senegal

CPSIA information can be obtained
at www.ICGtesting.com
Printed in the USA
FSHW010756171218
54527FS

9 781504 363723